I0445375

DREAM OUT LOUD

A SNEAKERHEAD'S
PATH TO REDEMPTION

BY RIKKI MENDIAS
& WENDY ADAMSON

Copyright © 2022 by Rikki Mendias and Wendy Adamson

All rights reserved.

ISBNs: 9798987093016 (hardcover), 9798987093009 (paperback), 9798987093023 (eBook)

Cover Design by Marc Alan Kropfl

Cover Photograph by Gabriel O'Neal

Photo Credits: Dez Jones, Rikki Mendias, Carlos Solorzano

CONTENTS

I've gotten more from giving out one pair of shoes than I ever did from owning hundreds.

—Rikki Mendias

PROLOGUE

Thanksgiving Day, 2018

It's 6:00 a.m., and I'm driving through Los Angeles, the city of fortune, fame, and possibility, when I find myself passing a homeless encampment. Tents, cardboard boxes, plywood, and blue tarps are lined up against a chain-link fence. You can go anywhere in this city, and eventually you'll come across an encampment of men, women, and children sleeping on the ground surrounded by their meager possessions.

I was once homeless when I was a kid, and it caused a perpetual feeling of being less than and a deep sense of shame. It ate at me for so long, I gradually bought into the idea that if I had enough material things, I'd somehow be equal to everyone else.

However, when I acquired those things, although they made

me feel all right for a minute, it never lasted. While most of my peers had ample opportunities, my mother was collecting welfare checks, so my own prospects were limited. I always had the underlying feeling that there was a world out there that I had no access to. The shame I felt all those years ago is just one of the things that motivate me to help others today.

I pull up to the Venice Beach basketball courts. The early-morning sun washes everything in a soft, pinkish-blue light. Seagulls circle overhead looking for their next meal. Shadows from the basketball hoops reach across the court, and the Pacific Ocean serves as a breathtaking backdrop. I feel the urge to get my basketball out of the car and take a few shots, but I see the line of homeless people forming, and I'm reminded there's work to do. Packed into the back of my Ford Flex are over two hundred pairs of sneakers I've brought from Hav A Sole, a nonprofit I started in 2014.

As soon as I step out of the car, I'm surrounded by volunteers. "Good morning, everyone. Thanks for coming out," I say. "Let's set the shoes out as fast as we can. Women's go on one side, men's on the other."

Our partner organizations are already setting up pop-up

tents that surround the courts, and other volunteers are arriving with an assortment of holiday food.

A half hour later, we are ready to go. "Let's huddle up, everyone," I say. "Just want to remind you guys that we are here to make everyone feel super special today. So give everyone an experience like they've stepped inside their favorite retail store."

Chairs are set up so that each person can try the shoes on. With Hav A Sole, no one walks away until they find something they like.

My mom comes up behind me and gives me a hug. "Do you need any help?"

"No, I think the volunteers have it under control." Mom is sixty years old now. Her hair is cut short, and she's super fit from hiking every day.

"This is amazing, Rikki. I'm so proud of you," she says.

I turn to face her. "Just think, none of this would have been possible if you hadn't gone to jail."

We both burst into laughter, which was not always the case.

ACT 1

SHOTS FIRED

It was May 17, 1991. I was nine years old and fast asleep on the living room couch.

I was woken up by a hand shaking my shoulder. I opened my eyes to a police officer standing over me. I was confused. My parents didn't like cops, so what was he doing inside my house? Lifting my head off the pillow, I wiped the sleep from my eyes. More sheriffs were rushing through the room; some headed down the hall while others went toward the dining room. There was a dull ache in the pit of my stomach.

The officer leaned closer, his belt full of black shapes. "I'm afraid we have to take you to the station with us, young man," he said.

"Why? What's wrong?" I searched his poker face for clues.

"Everything is going to be fine. Let's just get you a jacket."

I didn't trust him or the words coming out of his mouth. Nothing *felt* fine. I had a strong sense that something horrible had happened, and I wanted to know what it was.

The officer followed me into my bedroom, where I grabbed several G.I. Joe figures and stuffed them inside my jacket pocket and then slipped on my favorite pair of Nikes.

Moments later I stepped onto the front porch, but it felt like I had wandered onto the set of a Hollywood movie. Dozens of police cars were parked in the middle of the street. Red and blue lights streaked across my face. Nothing seemed real.

I don't remember being put in the squad car. I don't remember the drive to the police station. I don't remember anything ever being explained to me. What I do remember is sitting in a small, bright room with fliers of wanted criminals plastered on the wall in front of me. My feet dangled over the side of a black swivel chair. I swung my legs back and forth, causing the chair to spin. A door buzzed down the hall and then it slammed shut. Loud voices got closer. I looked up just in time to see my mother, hands cuffed behind her back, being escorted down the corridor by two cops. She was arguing with them about something. My face turned hot. I wanted to call out to her, but I just sat there in silence. In that moment, I realized that something really, really bad must have happened, and whatever it was involved my mother. I was scared. I wanted to insist that someone tell me what was going on, but they had left me alone in that empty room. I hated not knowing. I hated the police. I hated being alone.

It seemed like hours before Dad finally showed up dressed in jeans, a Lakers sweatshirt, and white Adidas sneakers. "Are you okay?" he asked, gripping my arms.

"What's happening to Mom? What are they doing to her?"

His eyes darted around like he was scared someone would hear us. "Shhh. It's okay. I'll tell you when we get to the car."

He led me by his clammy hand down a dimly lit sidewalk to a white El Camino with a narrow camper shell on the back. I recognized the car immediately. It belonged to Kim, my parents' new friend who sometimes hung out at our house for hours. She was sitting shotgun, her long blonde hair framing her face. "What is she doing here?" I asked.

"Just get in the car, Rikki."

I crawled over Kim to get in the middle. Dad went around

to the driver's side. That's when I noticed her right arm was wrapped in a sling and secured to her side. Dad sat with both hands on the wheel. "Your mom did something really bad tonight, Rikki."

"What? What did she do?"

He let out a long sigh. "When Kim and I came back from the store, I was looking for a parking space, and your mother came out of the house with a gun. She fired two times, and one of those bullets hit Kim in the arm."

It felt as if some invisible hand was squeezing my heart. "But why? Why would she do that?" None of it made any sense.

"I think she lost her mind, son."

I looked over at Kim, then back to my dad. My thoughts spiraled to a dark place. *If Mom had lost her mind, would she ever be able to get it back again? What if she went to one of those prisons I had seen on TV? What if I never saw her again?*

THE DAY AFTER

Once home, exhaustion set in and I fell asleep, but the next morning, I woke up to the sound of voices in the other room. "Mom did what?" My big brother's voice echoed down the hall. I rushed into the living room, still in my pajamas. Jerry was seventeen, eight years older than me. His T-shirt revealed thick arms defined from weight lifting. Dad and Kim were sitting next to each other on the couch. I didn't like that she was still there, but I didn't say anything.

"Did you hear what Mom did?" Jerry asked.

"Yeah. The cops woke me up last night."

"No fucking way." He shook his head in disbelief. "What the fuck, Dad? What made her do that?"

"Like I told Rikki, we were looking for a parking spot when

I heard what sounded like a gunshot go off behind me." Dad pointed to the street. "After I turned the corner, I stopped the car trying to figure out what the hell was going on." He shook his head. "Then all of a sudden, your mom jumps out and lays across the hood, pointing a fucking gun at me. I thought she was going to kill me, so I stepped on the gas. When she slid off the car, she fired another round, and it hit Kim in the arm." Dad gave Kim a sympathetic look.

"No. Fucking. Way," Jerry said.

"Your mother was always afraid she'd end up like her mom, who was mentally ill," Dad said, shaking his head.

A heaviness gripped my chest. I had no real understanding of what was happening, but I knew one thing—I was mad. I was mad at Mom for turning everything upside down. I wanted answers. I wanted to know why she would do something so stupid to get herself locked up.

A CALL FROM COUNTY

I stopped going to school. I kept asking Dad what was going to happen to Mom, but all he said was, "I don't know, son." Our phone had been disconnected, so she couldn't call, and without any answers, my mind created a dark place inside me.

I wanted to take my entire family somewhere we could be like other families whose mothers cooked dinner and everyone sat down for a family meal. I wanted to be the family who went to the beach or to Disneyland on our days off. I wanted to be the boy who felt safe and who knew that, no matter what, his parents would make everything all right. But I was afraid that things would never be all right again.

Several days after that horrible night, I was alone in the living room when I heard a tapping on the sliding glass door that led out to the pool area in the back. I peeked around the corner and saw Patty, our neighbor, waving at me. We were apartment managers, and Mom had rented Patty an apartment next door.

I slid open the heavy glass door with both hands.

"Hurry, hurry," Patty said. "Your mom is on my phone."

"What? She is? Where?"

"She's on my phone. Come on." Patty tugged on my arm.

Rushing next door, Patty pointed to the phone that laid on the countertop. I picked it up. "Hello?" I said.

"Rikki? Hi, hi, sweetie."

The sound of her voice pulled at my heart. "Where are you at, Mom?"

"I'm in jail." She sighed. "But as soon as I get everything straightened out, I'll come back home. I promise."

I shifted my weight. "How long is that going be?"

"I don't know yet, but soon." There was a pause. "Is your brother mad at me?"

"He doesn't want to talk to you anymore."

"You both have every right to be mad at me. I really messed up, Rikki."

I didn't respond. Feelings of powerlessness, anger, and sadness swirled inside me like clothes tumbling in a dryer.

"Rikki, I love you so much."

Again, I didn't say anything.

"Rikki?"

"I don't know if I love you anymore, Mom. Why did you try to shoot Dad?"

"I . . . I didn't know the gun was loaded."

I knew she was lying. "Then why did you shoot twice?"

"I'm so sorry, Rikki." Her voice cracked.

A jail recording came on: "This call will be disconnected in thirty seconds."

"I love you, Rikki."

I couldn't bring myself to tell her I loved her. I couldn't let her off the hook. I was tired of all her excuses and all the *I'm sorrys* she had been laying on me for the past year: "I'm sorry I was late picking you up from school." "I'm sorry we can't go to the park today." "I'm sorry I'm too busy to play right now." And although I wouldn't find out until much later that all this was a direct result of both my parents doing drugs, in that moment it was my mom who had abandoned me.

I hated her for that.

EVICTED

Three weeks later, Dad stood in the doorway of my bedroom in his boxers, the tattoo of Mom's name etched across his heart. The somber look on his face told me he had more bad news. "We have to move, Rikki."

"What do you mean?" I bolted straight up.

"We're getting kicked out."

"But why?"

"The owner wants us out."

"Does he know Mom went to jail?" Everything bad that was happening in my life seemed to circle back to Mom.

"Yeah. I think he knows everything." Dad stepped into my room and looked around at all the Legos scattered across the floor. "You're going to need to get rid of some of your things,

Rikki, because we can't keep everything in storage."

"But I don't want to get rid of my stuff." I had a chest full of toys, and my closet was filled with even more.

"We don't have a choice, Rikki."

"But what about all my G.I. Joes? And my Transformers?"

"You can keep those."

"Where are we going to go?"

"I don't know yet." Shoulders slumped, Dad turned and walked away. A lump of fear stuck in my throat.

The furniture went first. Dad sold Mom's expensive antique armoire to one of his friends. The television set in my parents' room disappeared. Bit by bit, the house was emptied of all our belongings. I was afraid to go anywhere, because when I came back, something else would be gone. I planted myself on my bed and stared at the ceiling, wishing I could be the one who disappeared.

***

Early one morning, Jerry and I were sitting in the kitchen. He had to go to court to face a vandalism charge he had gotten months before. "Are you scared about what's going to happen today?" I asked.

"I'm hoping I don't get locked up." He stared into his cereal bowl, his brow creased with concern.

"But what if you do?"

He shrugged. "Not much I can do."

The plan was that Aunt Armida, Dad's sister, would accompany him to court for moral support. We had just finished eating when she arrived. "We've got to hurry. I don't want to be late," she said, her purse dangling from her arm.

"Hi, Tia Mida," I said.

"Hi, sweetie." She leaned over and kissed my cheek. "Sorry I'm in such a hurry, but the 405 is a mess at this time."

Jerry and I hugged and said a quick goodbye. I convinced myself I'd see him later, but he never came back. The judge sent him to juvenile hall, and now I was the kid with two family members locked up. That night when I laid in bed, I inhaled deeply, trying to push back the tears. At nine years old, I already knew boys weren't supposed to cry, so whatever sadness I felt was locked inside a vault as I willed myself to go numb.

Things happened pretty quickly after that. Dad moved boxes filled with what few belongings were left into an eight-by-ten storage unit. I kept about half a dozen G.I. Joes and Transformers, along with enough clothing to get me through a week. I don't remember Dad giving me any explanation of what was going to happen next, but I do remember standing in the driveway looking inside the back of the camper shell on Kim's El Camino with the thin mattress covering the floor. "We're going to have to stay in here for a while, son," Dad said.

"What? But it's too small." I couldn't believe I was going from having my own bedroom to being cramped inside the back of a car.

"Don't worry, it's only temporary."

Dad must not have known that I worried all the time now. I worried about Mom. I worried about my brother. I worried that my life would never be the same again.

DISPLACED

Living in the car, I'd have to wear the same wrinkled, dirty clothes every day. I was embarrassed and told Dad I didn't want to go to school looking like a bum, and he didn't seem to object, so I didn't go. Whenever I had to brush my teeth or wash my face, he'd take me to a public bathroom, but I still felt dirty after washing up in the sink. During the day I'd sit with Kim and Dad parked on a random street or in front of one of their friend's houses with nothing to do but wait. I never knew what we were waiting for, but sometimes it felt like were waiting for night to come so that I could go in the back and fall asleep.

***

One night we pulled into a small parking lot behind Joe's bar where Dad used to love to drink, play pool, and shoot the shit, as he used to say. It was dark outside, and I was curled up in the back when Dad opened the hatch. "I'll be back in a little bit," he said.

"Where are you going?" My eyes were filled with sleep.

"Inside the bar."

"But for how long?" Starting to panic, I sat up on my elbow.

"I'll just be a few minutes."

"Please hurry back, Dad. I don't like it here."

After that, I couldn't sleep. Booming music from a jukebox drifted out from the back door of the bar. An orange security spotlight shined through the car's windows. The air inside the shell smelled of body odor, bad breath, and cigarette smoke. I kept peeking out the window looking for Dad. What was supposed to be minutes turned into an hour. I flinched at every noise. I was afraid that any minute a stranger would open the hatch and kidnap me. I fought back the tears. *What was Dad doing in there? What was taking him so long?* I wanted to be back in our house, snuggled in my cozy bed and surrounded by my favorite toys. A deep depression settled on me. I wanted my mom.

***

One day Dad said we were meeting Grandma and her new husband, Paul, at McDonalds. I was excited because I knew I'd get a Happy Meal with a toy inside. When I saw Grandma, I ran up to her and threw my arms around her. She had small white teeth, salt-and-pepper hair, and olive skin weathered from all her years of gardening in the sun. Paul had thick white hair and a handlebar mustache that curled up at the ends.

"Hi, *mijo*," she said, using a Spanish term of endearment.

"I've missed you," I said.

While I would see them during the holidays or family gatherings, they weren't a constant presence in my life.

After we ate, Paul wanted to go outside while Dad and Grandma talked. But when we got back to the table, Dad had more bad news. "Listen, son, you're going to have to stay with Grandma for a while."

I suddenly felt nauseous. "But I want to stay with you."

"It's for the best. We can't keep living in the back of the car."

The room tilted. I felt like I might fall to the floor. My entire family was being dismantled like pieces of a Lego set. I didn't trust any of the adults who were making decisions on my behalf. I wanted to run. But where would I go? Dad took me in his arms. "I'm sorry, Rikki."

The next thing I knew, I was sitting between Grandma and Paul in their truck. My lip quivered as Dad stood waving at me.

***

Grandma lived in a small yellow stucco house in Santa Monica. It sat behind a tall black wrought iron fence and had a garden filled with cacti and ceramic statues of cupids and gnomes. I carried my small bag of clothing into the living room, holding my jaw tight so I wouldn't cry. The smell of homemade tortillas and pinto beans seemed baked into the walls. Glass cabinets were arranged with angels, roosters, salt and pepper shakers, and ceramic dolls. I would soon learn that Grandma was obsessed with dusting and rearranging those collections all the time.

"You hungry, kiddo?" Paul asked. "Grandma will make us something else to eat."

"Yes, please," I said, even though I had just eaten.

The Hispanic women in the family always served the men

first. Mom never did that, probably because she was white.

While I waited for a burrito, I stared at the framed photograph of a younger, happier version of my family that hung on the wall. Mom was sitting front and center with straight brown hair. I was two years old and wearing corrective glasses for a lazy eye. My brother, Jerry, stood on one side, with my dad directly behind.

I studied the photograph as if by doing so, I could figure out what the hell went wrong with our family. Was it really all Mom's fault, or did Dad have something to do with it too? But mostly I thought I was the one to blame. Surely, there must be something I could say or do to get my parents back together again.

By the time we'd finished washing the dishes that night, it was nearly eight o'clock and time for bed.

"You'll be sleeping in here, Rikki." Grandma pointed to the black and tan couch in the living room. A clunky television sat in the corner, bookended by stacks of VHS tapes. Grandma showed me how to cover it with sheets and a comforter and told me I'd need to put the linens away every morning. "I'll leave the bathroom light on for you," she said.

"Thank you, Grandma," I said before disappearing down the hall.

What I remember most was the clock sitting on the mantel. It ticked. And ticked. And ticked. It would chime every hour, keeping me awake. My foot tapped endlessly while my mind raced with dark thoughts. *Will I ever see my parents again? Who's going to take care of me? Will I ever see Mom again?*

I'd never felt so alone. I was scared.

I closed my eyes. I was ready to leave this horrible dream, to wake up in my old bed, beneath my Spider-Man comforter, with my brother in his room and Mom and Dad in theirs.

FAMILY DAY

Sunday turned into Monday and then back to Sunday again. I was going to a new school, watching hours of television, and feasting on Grandma's burritos. Mom had been sentenced to a year for assault with a deadly weapon, but she said with good behavior, she could be out in nine months. It was around six months into her sentence when she called collect, excited about a new pilot program the county jail was trying out. "I got approved for you to come visit me," she said.

Up until that point, the county jail had only allowed kids to visit their mothers through a thick plexiglass window while talking on a tinny phone. The new program would allow kids to have direct physical contact with their moms, which was supposed to help with their well-being.

"So I can come to the jail?"

"If someone will bring you up here."

When Grandma was told of the new program, she thought it was a good idea and arranged for Dad to take me there. I had seen him once or twice since I went to Grandma's, but mostly we talked on the phone every week.

On the day of the visit, Dad picked me up in Kim's El Camino. When we embraced, he felt like all hard edges and bones, unlike the muscular version I had always known him to be while I was growing up. "You're so skinny, Dad."

"Well, thanks a lot, kiddo. And how've you been?"

"I've missed you."

"I miss you too, son. Are you happy to go see your mom today?"

It was confusing. On the one hand, I was excited, but on the other hand, I was still mad at her for leaving me. "Yeah. I am." I paused. "Don't you want to see her again?" I watched his reaction to see if there were any signs that he still cared for her.

"I sure do, kiddo," he said. "But I can't visit because of some stupid warrant I have for a parking ticket."

Dad was always getting tickets that he refused to pay, so this wasn't new.

Later, at the jail, Dad and I stood in a group with other families. On one side of the parking lot was an eight-foot wall with looped razor wire running along the top. A sheriff walked around, her head snapping back and forth like a prairie dog that had just popped out of a hole, watching everyone. The kids, mostly Black or Brown, were dressed up in what looked like their Sunday best. One chubby girl bounced up and down like she couldn't wait to get inside.

Finally, the lock released and the gate rolled open, revealing a group of women inmates on the other side.

"Enjoy your time with your mom," Dad said.

"Are you leaving?" I was nervous to go inside.

"I'll be back in two hours to pick you up. Tell your mom I said hi."

An officer stepped forward. "All right, kiddos. Time for your visits."

The kids hollered as they ran toward their mothers. I walked in slowly, scanning the women's faces until my eyes landed on Mom. She had put on some weight. Her brown hair cascaded in waves beyond her shoulders, like she had curled it for the visit.

I was surprised she looked better while she was inside jail. She rushed over. "Hi, sweetie. I'm so happy to see you." She hugged me and planted a wet kiss on my cheek.

My outward reaction was reserved. At nine years old, I had already learned how to conceal any emotions by acting cool. "Hi, Mom." I rubbed off the kiss with the back of my hand.

"I've missed you so, so much."

"I've missed you too." I leaned back, taking in her blue jump-suit.

"Is that what you have to wear?"

She jutted out her hip to one side. "Do you like it? It's the latest in prison attire."

Not getting the humor, I gazed beyond her shoulder. "So this is what a jail looks like? It doesn't seem so bad to me." There was a grass courtyard with a cluster of buildings in the corner. It in no way resembled the prisons that I had seen in the movies or on TV.

"This is the nicer area of the jail." Mom pointed to a dark-gray, windowless building behind us. "That's where we actually stay."

"Is it scary in there?"

"More depressing than scary."

"Do you have bars on your cell?"

"I'm actually in a dorm with over a hundred women. It's kind of like a big slumber party that you wish you didn't have to go to."

I laughed at the idea of women in pajamas having a slumber party behind bars. "Are there a lot of rules?"

"Too many to mention. You wouldn't like it here, that's for sure."

"What's all that for?" I pointed to the booths that had been set up for the day. One had an inmate ready to paint faces while another featured a ring toss game. It was strange seeing a mini carnival behind the razor wire and cinder block walls.

"You want to play one of the games?" she asked.

"Nah, I'm kind of tired. Can we just sit down for a while?"

"Sure. Whatever you want." We walked over to metal chairs and sat down.

"Dad told me to tell you hi."

"Oh he did, did he?"

"Yup."

"Do you see him very much these days?" Her tone got serious.

"Not so much, but he calls me all the time."

There was a long pause. "What happened to you after I went to jail?"

I hesitated. I didn't want to go into all that but felt like I didn't have a choice. "After we got kicked out of the apartment, I stayed in Kim's car with Dad until Grandma came and got me."

"What? You were living in her car?" Her brow got all scrunched up.

I shifted in my seat. I felt like she was interrogating me. "I don't want to talk about this anymore."

"Okay. I'm sorry, I'm sorry. I was just curious is all. How do you like your new school?"

"I don't like school." With all that had happened, my grades had suffered a lot. I had made a couple of friends, but I often got in trouble for goofing off in my classes. "When are you getting out, Mom?" It was the answer to this question that I really wanted to know.

"I have only a few more months to go."

We sat in silence and watched as a girl in a pink dress ran laughing across the grass as her mother chased after her. They seemed to be having so much fun. I thought back to a pool party we had in the backyard before Mom went to jail. My brother and his friends were there, and kids from the apartment complex joined in as well. Dad sat on a lounge chair smoking a cigarette as we cannonballed into the deep end of the pool. The backyard was full of splashing and laughing until, eventually, Mom brought us something to drink. "Come and get it, everyone," she called. "I have some fresh homemade lemonade here." She handed out red plastic cups to all the wet, dripping kids on the back porch. That was the last time I remembered having fun. Would it ever be like that again?

I couldn't help but wonder how the kids attending the family program felt about their moms being locked up. Did they miss their mothers as much as I did? As far as I could tell, there was no one in my school who had a mom in jail, but all these kids knew what it was like, and it didn't feel good.

"Where are we going to live when you get out, Mom?" I asked.

She looked down at her canvas tennis shoes. "I'm not really sure yet."

"You know we can't stay at Grandma's house. She told me

she doesn't have enough room."

"Trust me, I know. I will find us a place to stay."

After all we'd been through, I certainly didn't trust her anymore. To trust that she would magically find us a place to live from behind bars seemed like too much for anyone to believe. And by the ripe old age of nine, I never thought I could trust her again.

ACT 2

REUNITED

March 1992

When I opened the front door, Mom was standing there with her arms open, dressed in a bulky sweatshirt and jeans. A dark-haired woman with piercing blue eyes stood beside her.

"I'm so happy to see you, Rikki." Mom hugged me so tight, it felt like she gave me a chiropractic adjustment. "This is Candy, the person I told you about."

Mom had said during one of her collect phone calls that Candy was a teacher in the jail who belonged to a foundation that sometimes helped women find somewhere to live when they were getting out. Apparently, Candy wanted to help Mom.

She extended her hand. "Nice to meet you, young man. I've heard all about you."

"Nice to meet you."

I let them inside, where Grandma stood wearing one of her usual floral dresses, her long hair in braids that fell past her shoulders. "Welcome home, Wendy. You must be really happy to be out," she said. Paul stood behind her.

"Yeah, but I'm even happier to see Rikki." Mom smiled at me.

"You getting out of jail is all he's talked about for the last month," Grandma said.

While it was true that I couldn't wait to be with Mom, I was also worried about where we were going to stay. As if reading my mind, Grandma asked, "Any idea where you will be living?" I think Grandma really wanted her quiet lifestyle back, besides making it crystal clear that Mom needed to start taking on the responsibilities of motherhood.

Candy answered the question. "I've set up an interview tomorrow at a women's and children's center, but tonight they'll need to stay at a motel."

Grandma nodded. "Thank you so much for helping them," she said.

"I believe Wendy really wants to turn her life around."

"I hope so," Grandma replied. "Rikki really needs his mother."

Just then the phone rang, and Paul stepped aside to let Grandma answer it. It was Dad, and he wanted to talk to Mom.

Maybe he was going to ask Mom to get back together again. Maybe he had found a place for us to live. Maybe we could rewind all the VHS tapes to a happier time when there were loud voices and laughter at family dinners, beer cans hissing open, barbecues and pool parties, and sleepovers with friends. It felt like a spigot had opened and released a trickle of hope. I leaned in to hear Mom, but her tone didn't sound promising. "Don't worry," she said. "I've moved on with my life as well." By the time Mom sat back down, the spigot had closed.

Grandma handed me a lunch bag. "I made you a few of your burritos in case you get hungry later on."

"Thank you, Grandma."

Then she handed Mom a large brown bag full of my clothes. "When you get settled in your new place, you can come back for the rest of his stuff."

"I really don't know how I'll ever pay you back, Jenny," Mom said.

"Just stay sober and that'll be payment enough."

"I will. You'll see," Mom said.

33

***

Outside Grandma's house was a shiny red mustang with a black racing stripe. Candy pointed her keys at the car, and the alarm beeped twice. "This is your car?" My mouth dropped open. I couldn't imagine an old woman like Candy driving a souped-up car. She must have been over forty years old.

"Do you like it?" she asked.

"It's way cool." I climbed into the back seat.

"I got it as a birthday present for myself." She turned the key, and the engine roared to life. "Let's take her for a little spin, shall we?"

"Yes, please."

Driving toward the beach, it felt good to be in a fast car with the windows down. It had been boring living at my grandma's house.

Later, Candy checked us into the Palm Motel on Pico Boulevard. "I'll be back tomorrow morning to take you guys to your interview," she said.

The motel room was dark and depressing. It had thick blackout curtains, two queen beds, and a shower the size of a coffin.

Mom and I shared the burritos Grandma had made for dinner. I tried to watch television, but it had an automatic timer and kept shutting off.

"Why does it keep doing that?" I asked.

"I don't know." Mom was smoking on the other bed. I hated the smell of cigarettes. It clung to my nostrils, my eyelids, and my mouth. "When are you going to quit those nasty things?"

"Is it bothering you?"

"I can't breathe."

She took another drag before stubbing it out in the ashtray. I knew she felt guilty for everything that had happened, but I wasn't about to let her off the hook. "What if we don't get the place tomorrow?" I asked.

"Candy seems to think we will."

"And what happens after that?"

"I suppose I'll need to find a job."

Other than being an apartment manager, I hadn't seen Mom with a real job. "Doing what?"

"I don't know yet. Maybe I could be a receptionist."

"How will you get to work every day?"

"Take the bus until I have enough money to buy a car."

"You're not going to get a job or a car." I shot down her dreams like it was some new sport.

She sat up and flung her legs over the side of the bed. "Rikki, I know you're still mad at me, and you've got every right to be. But I'm sorry. Really, really sorry. I promise you things are going to be different now."

It was payback time. "I *really, really* doubt it." I turned my back and faced the wall.

***

The next morning, Candy drove us to the Clare Foundation offices, a rehabilitation center that offers support to recovering addicts. The hallway corridor was covered with slogans like "One Day at a Time" and "First Things First." Candy led us to an office where a woman sat, shuffling through papers on her desk. "Hi," Candy said. "We're looking for Ruth King."

"You've found her. Come on in."

Ruth was in her late fifties, but when she smiled, it took at least ten years off her face. Instantly I liked her. "Have a seat."

I sat down on the lumpy coach, and a puff of dust released into the air. My gaze landed on a bulletin board filled with photographs.

"Those are some of the women and children who have gone through our program," Ruth said. I smiled, wondering if my face would be plastered up there one day.

After some superficial chitchat, Ruth asked if she could talk to Mom alone for a few minutes. Candy and I went out to the parking lot. "You want to sit behind the wheel?" she asked.

"Really?" I crawled up into the soft black leather bucket seat. I put both my hands on the steering wheel and imagined myself driving. That was the kind of life I wanted. Fast, expensive cars with pockets full of cash.

A few minutes later, Mom called us back inside. "We have a place to live, Rikki," she said.

"We got it?"

"You sure did," Ruth said. "And you'll be sharing the two-bedroom apartment with Liz and her five-year-old son who has Down syndrome."

I had no idea what Down syndrome was, and I didn't care, just as long as we didn't have to sleep on the streets. Ruth explained that Mom could get on welfare, but eventually she'd need to get a job or go to school. The rent was only $400 a month, and Candy said her organization would cover the first two months.

"You'll have three mandatory meetings every week, Wendy," Ruth said before turning to me. "And while your mom's in the meeting, you'll get to play at our children's center next door."

For some reason, I liked Ruth, and while I wasn't thrilled about having more rules, I was grateful to have a place to live.

TRANSITIONAL LIVING

It was getting dark by the time we arrived at what would be our new home. We carried the bags of groceries Candy had bought us up the stairs. Mom tried knocking, but when no one answered, she used her shiny new key to get in.

Stepping into the living room, we found toys all over the floor, ashtrays spilling onto the coffee table, and a cracked mirror hanging above the couch. The walls were a dull shade of nicotine yellow, and the smell of rancid cigarette smoke permeated the air. I was surprised by how messy it was, but I knew better than to sound ungrateful when other people were around. I swallowed my disappointment and stepped over the toys. We made our way to the kitchen, where a landscape of dirty dishes was laid out in the sink.

"Your new roommate might need a little help with the dishes," Candy said. "Why don't we go check out your room?"

Our shared bedroom in the back had two unmade twin mattresses and mismatched dressers. The walls were bare except for a painting of a landscape that Mom would later hide in the closet. The brown carpet was so dirty, if anyone were to look any deeper, they might find a toenail clipping buried in there.

"It just needs a little bit of love," Candy said.

"And, Rikki, you can put up some Michael Jordan posters," Mom said.

I internally rolled my eyes, but what I wanted to say was it would take more than a few posters to spruce up that room. I don't know what I had expected, but I certainly didn't think I'd be sharing a room with my own mother. How embarrassing. If any of the kids from school found out, they would make fun of me. It was just one more thing I'd have to keep a secret from everyone else.

Candy said she had to get going in order to beat the traffic. "I'll check in with you next week," she said.

"Thanks for all your help," Mom said.

Mom then made us sliced turkey sandwiches on Wonder

Bread with red Kool-Aid to wash it down. Sitting at a small table, I was just shoving the last Dorito into my mouth when the door flew open.

Liz, our new roommate, had a square jaw and blonde hair with two inches of black roots. Her son, Jake, had slanted eyes and a large forehead. I would later learn these were features related to Down syndrome. When he saw me, he immediately grabbed my leg with both arms.

"Oh, stop that, Jake," Liz said. "I'm sorry, sweetie. When he sees another kid, he always wants to play."

Bending over, she loosened his little hands from my leg while I simultaneously gave Mom my best what-the-hell-have-you-gotten-me-into look.

THE WELFARE OFFICE

The first thing on Mom's to-do list was to get the welfare department to transfer over the checks from Grandma to us. While Grandma never had legal custody of me, the county still considered her my temporary official caretaker, and therefore she received benefits while Mom was in jail. When Mom told me I had to go, I rebelled. "I don't want to go to that smelly office," I said. I had gone with Grandma months before, and I had hated the place.

"In order to get paid, they have to see that you're back with me now."

When we arrived at the offices on Olympic Boulevard, mothers were standing out front smoking while their children played by their feet. I followed Mom through the cloud of thick smoke, holding my breath. We emptied our pockets into a plastic basket before heading through a metal detector. A security guard eyed everyone up and down. The lobby itself smelled of body odor and disinfectant. We stood in line until it was our turn.

"I'm here to apply for welfare," Mom said.

The clerk slapped down a clipboard and a pencil, barely looking up. "Fill this out and bring it back when you're done." She pointed a red manicured fingernail at some chairs.

Mom filled out the questionnaire while I played with Bumblebee, a yellow Transformer I had brought with me. I snapped, folded, and twisted the robot until it became a car and then twisted it back. Every few minutes I'd cringe at the sound of a baby's high-pitched scream piercing the air. A few minutes later, Mom let out a long, exasperated sigh.

"What's wrong?" I asked.

"I don't have a birth certificate or a social security card with me," she said. "I don't know where your dad put everything when he packed up what was left of my belongings."

I thought back to the horrible time when we were forced to move. Being evicted was so stressful, I'm sure Dad wasn't paying attention to where he put important papers.

Mom gave the form back to the clerk and then received a number. An hour passed, maybe two hours, until finally we were called to another window. I stood on my tippy-toes to see over the top of the counter. The cranky woman on the other side was rude. "Come back when you have the proper documentation," she snapped.

Not only did they want Mom to provide proper ID but also she needed to get someone like Ruth or Candy to write letters stating that she was sober now and fit to be a mother. Each time she went back, I had to go with her. I often wondered what people thought of us. The whole ordeal gave me more shame for having a mother who was too poor to support her own kid.

By our third month at Clare Foundation, the welfare situation hadn't been resolved. "I'm afraid we're going to be asked to leave if I can't pay the rent," Mom said, starting to panic.

"Where would we go?" I asked.

"I have no idea." She laid her head in her hands. "I didn't think it would be this hard."

During that time we were often short of food, so Mom had to go to a food pantry where she'd receive two bags of items ranging from day-old bread, a jar of Ragu, and perhaps some cereal that had already expired. We lived in such uncertainty, Mom started rationing food so that we could make it another week.

The constant stress of not having enough money or food made me angrier at Mom for getting us into this situation in the first place. I constantly compared myself to others, and when we walked through different neighborhoods, I'd look into the windows of all the nice houses. I wondered what their lives were like. I was convinced that there was no one who had it as bad as I did. It wasn't fair.

FATHER'S DAY

After my parents separated, Dad went from being a central figure in my life to me hardly seeing him at all. I had a secret dream that I held on to that one day my entire family would be back together again, but until that day, I just wanted to see him.

Whenever he called, I couldn't wait to talk to him. "When are you coming to see me?" I'd ask.

"I'll be there this Saturday," he said. "I promise."

The weekend rolled around, but Dad didn't up show again. Each time he didn't keep his word, I would get boiling mad, but the anger was directed toward my mom because she was the only one around. I would yell, kick a basketball, and slam the door to my bedroom before throwing myself on my bed. When Mom entered a few minutes later, trying to console me, I'd yell,

"Leave me alone!"

The following weekend Dad actually showed up, and I was shocked. Any resentments I had evaporated when I saw him swaggering up the pathway, with his dark shades and a baseball cap pulled down over his eyes.

"Dad, you came!" I ran up to him.

He gave me a big hug. "Of course I did. I needed to see my little man."

"I've missed you so much."

"I've missed you too," he said, looking up at Mom. "You're looking pretty good there, Wendy."

When he embraced her, my heart beat with expectation. *Maybe they liked each other again. Maybe it's not too late to get the family back together again. Maybe we can move out of this place and go somewhere nice.*

"So how do you like it here?" Dad asked.

"It's okay, I guess. But our roommates kind of suck," I said.

Mom smiled and nodded. "They do suck."

"At least you have a place to live," Dad said.

"We used to have a nice place to live before—" Mom stopped midsentence.

"Where are you living, Dad?"

"Kim and I are staying with some friends."

I cringed at the mention of Kim's name while Mom looked away. I may not have known a lot, but I knew that as long as she was around, my parents would never get back together again. I hated her for that.

We played catch all afternoon until Mom made us something to eat. Being with my mom and dad gave me a sense of peace. But I knew the feeling wouldn't last.

WET FEET

Sitting cross-legged on the floor, I slipped on my worn-out Payless shoes. I looked up at Mom, who was standing in the bedroom doorway. "I need new shoes, Mom."

"I told you, Rikki. I don't have the money right now."

"Can't you ask Grandma for some?"

"No. She already gave me money for school supplies."

"But look at these crappy things." The thin rubber had worn clear through the bottom of the sole, and the stitches of the seams were stretched apart.

"Maybe if we put a piece of cardboard inside."

"That's a stupid idea!" I couldn't believe she'd come up with such a lame solution. She had no idea what it was like trying not to be made fun of at school for your shoes, let alone someone finding out I had put cardboard in there.

Her brow creased in frustration as she reminded me that our welfare checks were barely enough to live on. I had heard the speech before, and while it always stirred my underlying resentment toward Dad for not giving us any money, it also made me angrier at Mom because she was the one reminding me in a thousand different ways that we were poor. At the time, I was convinced we'd always have to share a bedroom in a women and children's shelter and we'd always be using food stamps. I didn't know how to express my shame, so instead I blamed her.

"Let's get going or we'll miss the bus," she said.

I tossed my backpack over my shoulder. It took two buses to get to school, and I didn't talk the entire ride. She kept nudging me and trying to get me to smile, but I wasn't letting her off that easy. I used silence to let her know I was still mad. By the time we stepped off the bus, the sky had turned completely gray, and it looked like it was going to rain.

Mom pointed at my thin hoodie. "Are you going to be warm enough in that?"

I didn't answer her and instead ran onto the schoolyard.

While the homeroom teacher took roll call, my thoughts

drifted to my favorite sport: basketball. It was 1992, and the Chicago Bulls had just won their second championship. I believed all credit should have gone directly to the legendary Michael Jordan. He had such confidence in his own abilities on the court that no one could argue that when Michael played, he was all in. Not only was he my favorite player but also his shoes were my favorite sneaker. My older brother once told me that in 1984, when Michael debuted his red and black Air Jordans, the National Basketball Association tried to ban them because the colors weren't regulation. Jordan wore them anyway. Legend has it that's when the sneaker culture was born.

The sound of rolling thunder shook the classroom. A flash of lightning lit up the sky and sheets of rain came down. It poured all morning, but by the time the lunch bell rang, the rain had stopped, so we were allowed to go outside for recess. I joined the other boys on the wet court.

Basketball gave me a way to cope, but it also put me on a level playing field. I was agile, athletic, and fast. I could score a last-second game-winner or knock down a midrange jumper. The sound of feet pounding on the wet pavement and splashing through the puddles felt like freedom to me.

My tennis shoes screeched, and my muscles strained as I dribbled the ball toward the hoop. Another player got in front of me, shifting back and forth, waving his arms in front of my face. I easily dribbled past him and made the layup. This was where I got respect from other kids. My confidence grew whenever I was on the basketball court.

After recess, I noticed my socks were sopping wet from absorbing so much water. I shivered all through the afternoon classes. When the last bell rang, I was pissed off when I met Mom in front of the school.

"What's wrong?" she asked.

"My feet are soaking wet."

"But how did that happen?"

As far as I was concerned, it was her fault for not having money to buy me new shoes. "Let's just go," I said. I was in no mood to talk about it, and besides, she wouldn't understand.

Standing at the bus stop with my mom, I watched as a classmate rode by with his mother in a shiny new black Mercedes-Benz. I was convinced he was going to his fancy home with a swimming pool, his own room, brand-new toys, and his own TV. I wanted to be him. I wanted to be anyone but me.

BUY ONE GET ONE
HALF OFF

The shelter required us to follow certain rules. Among them, Mom had to attend a house meeting every Saturday morning with the other residents and staff while volunteers kept the kids occupied outside. My favorite volunteer was Phyllis. She had gray hair and a warm smile. The yard always had an assortment of broken, secondhand toys to play with. I had been tossing a football back and forth with Phyllis when my socks became saturated from the damp grass. I stopped playing and planted myself on the bottom step of the stairs.

Phyllis sat down next to me. "What's wrong, Rikki?"

I showed her the huge holes in the bottom of my shoes.

"Looks like you need a new pair," she said.

"Yeah, but my mom doesn't have the money."

"Have you tried the thrift store?"

Adults seemed to think it was okay to wear someone else's hand-me-downs. They didn't understand that sneakers were a status symbol and let others know who you were and where you'd been. Phyllis put a gentle hand on my back, trying her best to console me. While it was a nice gesture, I was convinced only a new pair of shoes would make me feel better.

An hour later, the meeting ended, and I burst into the room with one of my shoes in my hand. Mom was busy talking to a heavyset woman I had never seen before. "Mom, look at this." I held up my shoe near her face.

"Excuse me, Rikki. I'm talking to Becky here." Mom's face turned fifty shades of red.

"But I need new shoes."

Becky looked at me, then back to Mom. "If he needs shoes, I can buy him some," she said.

I knew Mom didn't like taking handouts, but I needed shoes. "Please, please, Mom?" I pleaded.

"Are you sure?" Mom asked Becky.

"We can go to the Van's store right now." Becky pointed toward the door.

Mom nodded and looked back at me. "That would be amazing."

I don't remember if I jumped up and down, but the thought of getting new shoes, even if they weren't Jordans, thrilled me. Vans were worn mostly by skaters, but I was sure I could still play basketball in them.

On the drive Becky shared about "hitting her bottom" and living in the transitional living center with her son. I thought it was really cool how she hadn't forgotten where she had come from. "The shelter saved my life," she said. "I feel like it's partly my responsibility to give back to the women and children who are there now." While giving back sounded like a noble cause, I didn't quite get it. All I cared about was acquiring a pair of new shoes.

We pulled up in front of the Vans store on the corner of Washington Boulevard, and there was a large red banner in the window that read BUY ONE AND GET THE SECOND PAIR HALF OFF.

"I guess you'll have to get two pairs, Rikki," Becky said.

"No way." It felt like I had just won the lottery.

Walking into the store, I was hit with the smell of factory-fresh shoes. I looked at all the different colors and styles lining the walls. A pair of black-and-white checkered slip-ons sat on a round display table. Becky grabbed a pair of classic black low-tops and said, "Why don't you try these on?"

I held the shoe up to my nose and inhaled the canvas and suede. The smell was like comfort food for my soul. "I like these a lot," I said.

"What size are you, young man?" the salesgirl asked.

"A size six."

A few minutes later, she was back with two boxes. I plopped down on the end of a wooden bench. The salesgirl knelt to assist me. I turned hot with embarrassment when I saw my big toe popping out of my sock.

"Might as well get some new socks while we're here," Becky said, handing me a three-pack.

After slipping on a fresh pair, I laced up the shoes. Smiling, I stretched my foot out in front of me, turning it back and forth like a windshield wiper. "These are so cool," I said.

"We should get a white pair as well." Becky winked.

The salesgirl came back with another box. "Do you want me to put these old ones in a bag for you?" she asked.

"Those can go in the trash," I said, glad to be rid of them.

For the first time, I couldn't wait to go to school on Monday to show off my new Vans. And from that day forward, needing new shoes would become my unhealthy obsession for years to come.

THE ROOMIES

I spent hours watching television growing up. One of my favorite shows, *The Fresh Prince of Bel-Air*, was about a single mom raising a street-smart kid from Philadelphia who decides to send her son to live with rich relatives in Bel Air. The prince literally gets plucked out of poverty and dropped into a privileged and luxurious lifestyle. What was even more cool about the prince was that every week he would rock next-level footwear and outfits on the show. Anything from 1990s high-tops to Timberland boots, not to mention his dope collection of Air Jordans.

Mom was on the couch behind me, and I was lying on the floor staring at the TV when Jake started pulling on my pajama sleeve. "Play. Play. Play," he chanted.

"Not now, Jake. I'm busy."

Liz was in the hallway on the phone, her high-pitched voice

echoing off the walls, completely oblivious to what was happening with me and her son.

Jake stomped his foot again. "Play!"

Just then, Mom spoke up on my behalf. "Rikki's watching something right now, Jake. He'll play with you later."

He would not stop bugging me, so I went to sit next to Mom, hoping he'd go away. Absorbed in the unfolding drama of the show, I never noticed Jake as he got up on the coach and came along side me, sinking his tiny teeth into my shoulder.

"Owwwwww!" I jumped up so fast, Jake lost his toothy grip.

"What the hell?" Mom yelled.

Liz must have heard the ruckus because she came rushing in. "What's going on?"

"Jake just snuck up on Rikki and bit him." Mom turned me around to show Liz the tiny teeth marks that were imprinted in my flesh.

"Oh my goodness. I'm so sorry, Rikki." She pointed a scolding finger at Jake. "You need to go to directly to bed, young man," she said before leading him by his hand toward their bedroom.

"That's it? That's all she's going to do to him?" I asked.

"He doesn't know any better, Rikki," Mom said.

"I don't care. I hate him. I'm *never* going to play with him again."

***

One evening, Liz was on the phone while Mom and I were watching TV, and Jake slipped out the front door once again. Whenever Liz became distracted, he would run down to the corner liquor store and try to take some candy off the shelf. We used to help her with these frantic searches, but after he bit me, I didn't care if he disappeared forever.

"I think Jake is gone again," Mom said.

The phone slammed down into the receiver, and Liz rushed into the room. "Where did he go?" Her eyes darted around the room.

"I have no idea." Mom shrugged. "He was here a minute ago."

"Jake? Jake? Where are you?" Liz ran out the front door.

Mom did an eye roll while I just shook my head.

Several minutes passed before Liz came back, dragging Jake by the hand. "You guys could have stopped him from leaving," she said.

Mom could be easygoing until she'd enough, and this was one of those times. Narrowing her eyes as if in some sort of Mexican standoff, Mom said, "You might try watching your own kid instead of talking on the goddamn phone all the time."

Liz's hand shot up to her mouth. "How dare you!"

"Seriously, Liz. It's the same damn thing every night."

"You have no idea what it's like having to raise a handicapped son," she said. "Rikki will never experience the things that Jake will have to go through."

"That doesn't mean we should be responsible for him." Mom stood up. "Come on, Rikki. Let's go."

I followed Mom to the bedroom, and she slammed the door behind us. Sitting down on our twin beds across from each other, I asked, "When can we get out of this place?"

"If I had the money, we'd already be gone."

***

The small bathroom had a toilet behind the door as well as an oversize sink, and to turn on the faucet in the tub, you had to squeeze around the cabinet and reach your arm through the frosted sliding glass door. Because it was so awkward, Mom always did it for me. "Your bath is ready," she called from the other room.

I didn't want to take a bath, but I cooperated because *The Fresh Prince of Bel-Air* was on again that night, and I didn't want to miss it.

After Mom left me alone, I got undressed and was about to step into the tub when I saw something weird. Leaning over, I squinted at what looked like a Baby Ruth candy bar floating in the water, only it was a piece of shit.

"Mom! Mom! Come in here." I wrapped the towel around my waist.

Mom stuck her head inside the door. "What's going on now, Rikki?"

"Look inside the tub."

Mom stepped in and gazed beyond the frosted glass. "Oh hell no," she said. "Jake must have shit in the tub."

"That's so disgusting. I'm not taking a bath now."

"Just put your pajamas on."

"Mom, we need to move."

"I know, Rikki. I'll talk to Ruth King. Maybe she can help us."

HOME SWEET HOME

Six weeks later, when Mom picked me up at school, the first thing she did was show me a key sitting in the palm of her hand.

"What's that?" I asked.

"Ruth King says there's an apartment available if we want it."

"Our own place?"

"Yes, but we have to go see it first."

"Are you kidding? When?"

"Right now."

Eleventh Street and Pico Boulevard was a busy intersection several blocks away from my school. When we got to the two-story beige complex, Mom said the unit was upstairs.

I ran up, taking two steps at a time, as Mom followed behind.

She used the key to let us in, and the first thing I saw was several small coffee tables stacked on top of each other in the center of the living room. The apartment smelled of fresh paint, and on the right was a kitchen. Mom opened and closed the cabinets. She turned on the water and looked under the sink.

"Let's go see the bathroom."

The bathroom wasn't much bigger than the one we were using. "It's a bit small, but at least there's no shit in the tub," she said.

I laughed.

The bedroom was tucked in the back corner. It wasn't the biggest room, but the closet took up an entire wall.

"Would we have to share it again." I gazed up at Mom.

Mom smiled. "No, kiddo. You need a room to yourself," she said. "I'll get a futon and sleep in the living room."

I threw my arms around her. "I love you, Mom. When can we move in?"

"Right away."

Although it might not have been Bel Air, things were definitely looking up.

FATHER FIGURE

Mom's new sober life required her to attend a lot of recovery meetings, which was fine by me, but as an eleven-year-old, I had never done drugs, so I didn't see why I should have to go. "Can I just stay home?" I asked.

"The house rules require you to have a babysitter."

Mom had always been a rule-breaker, and the thought of having a babysitter seemed ridiculous after everything I had been through in the past two years. I couldn't figure out why all of a sudden she was trying to be a saint.

"We can go to the promenade afterward."

Since she was trying to bribe me, I used it as an opportunity to negotiate better terms. "Will you buy me some shoes?"

"Rikki! You know I don't have any money right now."

This was Mom's typical response anytime I wanted something, and I was sick of being reminded of just how poor we were. In my mind not having money meant everything would be secondhand from here on out. We'd never enjoy Disneyland like we used to. Movies with buttered popcorn were out of the question. Vacations to exotic islands were for other families to enjoy. My life had become nothing more than being in a constant state of deprivation, leaving me hungry for all the things I couldn't have.

When we got to the church where the meetings were held, groups of people were clustered out front. We had to pass through a thick cloud of smoke to get inside. "This place always stinks," I said as we shimmied through the crowd. Mom gave me one of those don't-even-start looks, but I didn't care. I wanted her to know how much I hated going.

The downstairs auditorium had rows of brown folding chairs already set up. I headed for the refreshment table and grabbed a fistful of cookies before joining Mom in our seats.

"Can we leave early?" I asked.

"We just got here," she said.

"Why do you go to these stupid meetings anyway?"

"To hear people tell their stories so I won't forget where I come from."

"That's just plain dumb."

We were interrupted when a loud voice boomed over the microphone. "Good evening," the leader said. "Can everyone please be quiet? The meeting is about to get started."

After reading some literature that I didn't understand, the leader introduced the first speaker, a tattooed hipster with a black-studded leather vest. As he began to "tell his story," the audience roared with laughter, but I didn't get any of the punch lines. What the hell was so funny about blackouts, getting arrested, and disappointing his family one more time? It all seemed stupid and beyond my comprehension. I was determined to let others know how I felt. The next time they laughed at one of his jokes, I said, "Ha ha!"

Heads turned to get a look at the bratty kid who was causing the disturbance while Mom's eyes narrowed into slits. "Stop it," she said.

"What?" I acted like I had no idea what she was talking about.

The next punch line, I was even louder. "Ha ha!"

71

Mom leaned over and whispered through tight ventriloquist lips, "You. Better. Stop."

"Can we go home then?"

"No, Rikki. We're not leaving."

By the time the break rolled around, Mom was so frustrated with me that she needed a cigarette. I followed her into the courtyard, where a sleek black-and-white Akita jumped up on my chest. The owner, a guy in a hoodie, pulled back on the leash. "Get down, Goldie," he said.

I knelt down beside the dog and ran my hand over his soft, thick fur.

"He really likes you," he said.

"I love dogs," I replied.

The man asked my name and reached out his hand and shook mine. "Hi, Rikki. I'm Gary Drake."

"Are you here for the meeting?" Mom asked.

"Yup, but I got here late, so I'm waiting for a friend."

"I hate those stupid meetings," I said, not holding back.

Gary laughed. "Yeah, sometimes they can be boring."

"Are you sober?" Mom said.

"Yup. I got sober at twenty-four."

"Really? How old are you now?"

"Thirty-six."

"How did you get sober so young?" Mom asked.

"It's kind of a long story." He paused. "But I grew up without a father figure and started to get into trouble when I was a kid. I spent years going in and out of juvenile hall and ended up in foster care. I was lucky, though, because I had a mentor who took me under his wing, or I probably wouldn't be here today."

Mom looked impressed. "That's an incredible story," she said and then asked what he did for a living. When he told her he owned his own construction business, she said, "Wow, very cool."

Just then a bell rang, indicating the second half of the meeting was about to start. Mom put out her cigarette under her foot. "Well, it was nice meeting you," she said, tapping me on my shoulder and indicating it was time to go.

"I don't want to sit through another speaker," I said.

"Rikki!" She shot me a look that said *don't embarrass me in front of this nice man.*

"He can hang with me and Goldie if you're okay with it," Gary said.

"Please, Mom," I begged. "Can I stay out here? Please?"

Mom looked from Goldie to me and then back to Gary. "Okay," she finally said, "but if you need me, you know where I am." She pointed inside through the floor-to-ceiling glass windows.

"We'll stay right here," Gary assured her.

"Can I hold Goldie's leash?" I asked.

"Sure thing, buddy, but you got to hold on tight."

My arm extended as Goldie pulled on the slack. "She's really strong."

"She is strong. Do you have a dog?" he asked.

"I can't have one where we're living."

"Oh, that's too bad."

"Yeah. It sucks."

For the next thirty minutes, Gary and I talked about Nintendo, the kinds of movies we liked, and our hobbies. Gary was funny and much more entertaining than any meeting might have been. "Do you roller blade?" he asked.

His question made me feel like we were kindred spirits. "I love it!" I said. "But I've only done it at the Boys and Girls Club."

"Oh man," he said, almost sympathetically. "You've never

bladed the bike path?"

I explained to him how that wasn't an option because Mom couldn't afford to buy me my own pair of roller blades. He nodded with a pensive look on his face.

Our time together seemed to fly by because suddenly the meeting was over and Mom was back by my side. "Thanks for hanging out with Rikki," she said.

A girl with wavy hair came up and gave Gary a quick peck on his cheek. "This is my friend Susie," he said by way of introduction.

Mom apparently knew Susie from other meetings. "Hey, Susie. Nice to see you," she said.

They talked a few minutes, and we were about to leave when Gary asked Mom, "I was wondering if I could come over and play Nintendo with Rikki sometime? You know, hang out with him a bit."

I knew Mom didn't like to have people over because our apartment was decorated with thrift shop bargains, but I really wanted to spend time with Gary. "Please, Mom?" I begged for the second time that evening.

Mom shifted uneasily. I knew I had put her on the spot.

"Give me call and we can talk about it," Mom said, writing down our number.

I would find out later on that Mom did a little investigative work on Gary, and it turned out they had many of the same friends. The word was that Gary could be trusted. In fact, everyone loved him, so Mom said he could come over that following weekend.

On Saturday when he showed up, I was excited to see him. "Do you know how to play *Bases Loaded*?" I asked.

"Are you kidding? That's my favorite game."

Mom had hooked up the Nintendo to the living room TV, so we sat on the floor, thumbs dancing on our controllers, manipulating a realistic pitcher, batter, and teammates on the screen. Instantly, we launched into a fierce competition. The virtual crowd cheered and hollered whenever we scored a run. We played for two hours straight while Mom stayed in the kitchen. Eventually, it was time for Gary to leave.

"Thank you for coming over to see Rikki," Mom said.

"We had a lot of fun," he said. "I was wondering if I might be able to take him roller blading on the boardwalk some time?"

Hanging out with Gary would be much more fun than staying inside our small apartment, so I pleaded with Mom to agree.

Mom looked at me before caving in. "Sure. Why not?"

The following Saturday I was so excited, I got dressed early. But then a dark thought crossed my mind. What if he doesn't show up? That was my experience with my dad. But thankfully Gary was as good as his word. When he knocked on the door at 10:00 a.m. as promised, my fear disappeared.

"Where are you guys going?" Mom asked.

"I thought we'd rent some skates in Santa Monica and roll on down to Venice."

"When will you be back?" she asked.

"How does four o'clock sound?"

"Perfect."

We headed toward the beach in Gary's cool SUV. "What kind of music do you want to hear?" he asked.

"I like rap music."

"How about some 2Pac?" He turned up the volume and tapped the steering wheel like it was a drum.

At the Santa Monica pier, the smell of hot dogs and mustard from the food stand lingered in the air. Gary had me fitted for roller blades at a rental stand. "Do you want knee pads?" he asked.

"No. I don't need them." I didn't want to be encumbered by anything that might slow me down.

After I put on the sleek black blades, I stood up while Gary put on his own pair. He smiled. "Let's see what you can do."

I wanted to impress Gary with the moves I had learned at the Boys and Girls Club. I did a 180, sending the whole world spinning around me.

"Dude, you're pretty good," Gary said.

"Let's go," I said, tightening my thigh muscles, tucking my arms into my ribs, and heading down the bike path. As I picked up speed, I could hear the ball bearings spinning in the wheels as the ground rushed beneath me. As my heart thumped louder, I felt like a human bullet cutting through space and time. Instead of being stuck inside playing video games all day, I was out in the world having fun.

Gary and I bladed every weekend for months. Hanging out with him was like being with a big brother or a best friend. He made me laugh all the time. One day when he picked me up, he surprised me by saying, "Let's get you your own roller blades today."

We went to a sports store where Gary picked out a black pair with red trim. "What do you think of these?" he asked.

"Those are cool." I ran my hand over the shiny plastic.

"Can we get a size eight?" Gary asked the clerk.

It reminded me of when Becky bought me two pairs of Vans. At the time I couldn't quite grasp the generosity of the individuals who were showing up in my life, but he was helping to fill the hole left by my MIA brother and dad.

When the clerk came back, I slipped the blades on. "These are awesome," I said, standing up and shifting back and forth. "I love them."

During my time in transitional living, I had watched my friends hanging out with their families on the weekends. With Gary showing up every week, it helped to ease the sting of missing out on my own family outings. I didn't know it yet, but Gary's influence would one day change the course of my life.

BROTHER LIKE MOTHER

One day when I arrived home from school, Mom was sitting on the couch smoking a cigarette. At eleven I could already feel the weight of her sadness hanging in the air. "What's wrong?" I asked.

"Your brother got arrested."

My stomach tightened. "For what?"

"Assault with a deadly weapon."

I flashed back to the night Mom went to jail for the exact same thing. It felt like history was repeating itself with my brother.

"What happened?"

"He was at a party and got into an argument, and the guy pulled a knife on him. He wrestled it away and stabbed him with it."

It was no secret that Jerry had a lot of pent-up rage stemming from his childhood. It would be stupid for anyone in their right mind to mess with him. "Is the guy all right?"

"Yeah. Thank God."

"What's going to happen to Jerry?"

"He's eighteen, so he'll probably end up going to state prison this time."

While the thought of my big brother doing hard time was frightening, once again there was nothing I could do.

***

The phone rang a few weeks later, and it was my brother calling collect. Mom held the receiver out from her ear so that I could hear what was being said. "You're not going to believe this, but Dad's in the same cell with me," Jerry said.

I leaned closer to hear.

"What do you mean?" she said.

"He got arrested on a warrant, and they put him in the same cell."

"Holy crap."

After she hung up, Mom seemed to collapse on the coach.

"What's going to happen to them?" I asked.

"They'll both probably get time." She placed her face in her hands.

I didn't have the words needed to console her, so to stave off the wrecking ball of sadness, I retreated to my room to play video games. On the bed, my thumbs danced across the control pad as I made the Mario brothers exterminate all the creatures emerging from the sewers by knocking them upside down or kicking them away. Although I couldn't control my family's fate, at least I had some control over the two brothers on the screen. I'd play for so long that my legs would fall asleep. Whenever I reached the highest level, I'd take a deep breath and feel a fleeting sense of relief. And then, in my mind, I'd imagine my brother and dad cramped inside a small cell together. Fear gripped my throat.

Am I going to end up being just like them?

FOLLOWING IN THEIR FOOTSTEPS

Two years later, the automatic doors of Macy's opened, and I headed straight for the men's cologne on the first floor. I was dressed in cargo shorts and black Vans, and I had a lemonade in one hand and a brown shopping bag in the other. At thirteen, I was convinced if I doused myself with the right cologne and had on dope sneakers, more girls would be attracted to me.

"Can I help you, young man?" the saleswoman asked.

"No, thank you. I'm just looking."

"Let me know if you need anything," she said before turning her attention to another customer.

I picked up a bottle on the counter, sprayed it in the air, and leaned into the mist. It was way too flowery, so I grabbed the Hugo Boss and sprayed it directly on my neck. I loved the sweet, leathery fragrance and the white frosted bottle it came in. But instead of putting it back on the counter, I casually let it slip into my shopping bag. My heart was pounding so loudly, I could hear it beating inside my brain.

I had only stolen a couple of time before, but whenever I did, my mind shifted into a hypervigilant state, observing and analyzing my surroundings. I was in that zone as I walked toward the exit, my eyes scanning for any potential threats. When I made it out of Macy's door, I thought I was in the clear, but before I got to the main exit of the mall, a plainclothes security guard with angry eyes grabbed my arm. My lemonade slipped from my hand and splattered all over our shoes, making him even more upset than before.

"Give me your bag," he said.

"Why? What did I do?"

"Give it to me." He snatched it from my hand.

Looking inside, he saw the cologne. "So you think you can come in here and steal whatever you want?"

I tried to formulate an answer that would explain how the Hugo Boss cologne jumped into my shopping bag, but I was at a loss for words.

"Come on, kid. You're coming with me." He led me back inside the store.

It was humiliating to see all the heads turning in disgust as the young hoodlum, who happened to be me, was escorted upstairs. Even store employees scowled and shook their heads as I went by. When we reached a back office, the security officer told me to sit down.

He gazed at me. "Have you done this before?"

"Never," I lied.

"What possessed you to take something that doesn't belong to you?"

"I wasn't thinking," I said, which was another lie. My thinking was more along the lines of going to any lengths to get what all the other kids at school had. But of course I didn't say that.

There was a long silence. "Well, it's your lucky day, kid. I'm not going to call the police, but you will never step inside a Macy's store again."

My chest caved in with relief. "Okay, okay, I promise. Never again." I would have agreed to anything at that point.

"You'll need to get one of your parents down here to pick you up."

"But . . . but I don't know my mom's work number by heart," I said. Those were the days before everyone had cell phones.

"What about your father?"

"I don't know where my dad is."

"You must have some relative who can pick you up." His tone was softening a bit.

"I suppose I could call my grandma." While I didn't want to tangle her up in my mess, I didn't have a choice.

He pointed to a black phone on the desk. "Get her down here, or I'll be forced to call the police." As I pushed the buttons, dread pulsed through my veins.

It rang about six times before she answered. "*Bueno?*" she said.

"Grandma? Hi, it's Rikki. I need a ride."

"Where are you, *mijo*?"

"At Macy's. The security guard won't let me go unless someone picks me up."

"Did you take something from the store?"

"I'm sorry, Grandma."

"Oh Rikki. Why would you want to do that?"

"I was stupid, I guess."

"I'll get Paul to drive me down there."

An hour dragged by before Grandma arrived. When I saw the look of disappointment on her face, a feeling of shame rippled through me. They drove me home in silence, and when she let me out in front of the apartment, she said, "I'll give you time to explain to your mom what happened, but I'm going to call her tomorrow to follow up."

Later, when Mom got home from work, we sat at the kitchen table. Her eyes widened and her brow creased. "Do you want to end up like your brother and father, in and out of jail?" she asked.

When I didn't respond, she took a deep breath before exhaling slowly. My head lowered on its own. We were close enough that I could sense her fear and frustration, but I also knew she blamed herself. I wanted to do better, I really did, but I didn't have a clue as to how to go about it.

"You can't do this shit, Rikki, or you'll end up just like them."

Hearing the desperation in her voice triggered a defense mechanism, and along with that came the familiar feeling of resentment. I often imagined how my life might have been different if my family hadn't been so fucked up, and in many ways, I blamed my mom for that.

EASY MONEY

When I started Santa Monica High School, I had big dreams my freshman year, but not the kind of dreams that involved academic achievements. My goal was to make money so that I could acquire the fresh sneakers everyone else had. The way I planned to do this was by selling weed. When a friend introduced me to a drug dealer, I bought my first four ounces. I quickly learned that my immediate challenge would be to keep myself from smoking up all the profits, and since I never paid attention in any of my math classes, I didn't know how to correctly measure the product.

Since my house was the closest to school, my friends would come over before class. Mom left early for work, so I didn't have to worry about her being in my business. When Dominic, Chris, and Elijah arrived, they brought the biggest blunt I had ever seen.

"Let's go so we have enough time to smoke this shit," Dominic said.

"Give me a minute." I quickly stuffed three ounces of weed into my backpack. It was packaged and ready for sale. I figured I'd just sell it in bulk to move it quicker. As we walked down the alley, Dominic, who had a finely trimmed chinstrap goatee, lit up and passed the blunt around. We talked about sports, upcoming parties, and, of course, girls.

"Did you hear about Charlotte?" Dominic asked, taking a hit.

"No, what about her?" I replied.

"She got caught having sex in one of the school bathrooms."

"Oh shit. I'm okay with that."

What I had picked up so far from my friends was to act like you knew everything you needed to know about girls. I pretended I had a lot of sex, but in reality I was still a virgin. What little I did know came from watching porn or looking at dirty magazines, but I pretended like I had done it all.

Dominic seemed to have a handle on the whole sex thing. I was convinced it was his facial hair that attracted all the girls.

That's why I started shaving the peach fuzz on my face to see if I could catch up with him. So far, it hadn't worked.

A few blocks from Santa Monica High, we were smoking the last of the blunt. We were just about to cross the street when Mr. Cooper, the school security guard, pulled up in his three-wheeler patrol cart. He had dark pockmarked skin and wore a uniform that looked like the ones worn by the Los Angeles County sheriffs. "Hold it right there, boys!" he yelled.

"Oh shit," I said, flicking the rest of the blunt under a car.

"You guys are late," he said, scanning the area around us. "What is this?" He bent over and picked up a small two-inch pipe that someone had dropped. "I want all of you to sit down on the curb." He pointed.

I followed orders, but the voice inside my head told me to get out while I still could. If I got caught with three ounces of weed in my backpack, I'd probably go to juvenile hall. I looked directly into Elijah's bloodshot eyes and whispered, "I'm about to run."

"What?" he said, raising an eyebrow.

I mouthed the words more slowly. "I. Am. About. To. Run." I pushed myself up and sprinted down Ninth Street faster than a track star.

Mr. Cooper yelled behind me, "Hey! Stop! Get back here!"

I cut in between two apartment buildings and made it to an alley. I was still two blocks from home when I squatted behind a car. Out of breath, my mind felt like a swarm of wasps were buzzing around. *Should I stash my weed or try to make it home?* I didn't hesitate for long. I left the alley and came out on Pico Boulevard, making it home in a few minutes.

Safely inside with the door locked behind me, I put the weed in five layers of Saran Wrap, packaging it up tight. I then put it into two ziplock bags and stashed the weed under my dresser. If the cops came, I figured they wouldn't look there, and I didn't want Mom to find it because ever since she had gotten sober, she had developed a keen sense of smell.

I spent the rest of the day worrying about what had happened to my friends. I imagined Mr. Cooper was probably trying to get them expelled. To distract myself I hopped on my Game Boy. When Mom got home from work, she was all up in my face. "What happened at school today?" She scrunched her forehead.

Oh shit, she already knows, I thought.

"What do you mean?" I feigned innocence.

"The principal wants to see us tomorrow morning at eight a.m. sharp."

"He does?"

She put her hand on her hip. "What happened, Rikki?"

"The security guard stopped me and some other kids."

"But why did you run?"

"They were smoking weed, and I didn't want to get in any trouble."

I don't think she believed me. "We'll see what the principal has to say about this tomorrow," she said.

Inside the principal's office, Mr. Cooper was also there, with his arms folded across his chest. I kept my head down, wondering why he was at the meeting. The principal, a white-haired middle-aged man, looked stern. "What happened yesterday, Rikki?" he asked.

"Um, I was walking to school when Mr. Cooper stopped me and a group of guys, and he found a pipe in the grass. It wasn't mine, and I thought I was going to get blamed for it."

"Were you smoking marijuana?" the principal asked.

"No, I wasn't."

"Then why did you run?"

"Because I didn't want to get in trouble."

"That wasn't your pipe?" Mr. Cooper asked.

"No. It was already there."

I tried my best to look outraged and offended, but I could tell by his stony eyes that he wasn't buying it. However, with no real evidence to pin on me, all I received was Saturday detention.

Later, when I met up with the guys, they told me they had gotten off as well because Cooper couldn't prove the pipe was theirs.

"Did you see how fast I ran?" I said.

"You were zigzagging all over the place. I could have jogged and caught up with you," Dominic said.

"Oh man, I was really zigzagging? I must have been really high."

We all laughed. I felt a sense of pride not only for getting away with it but also because I had managed to keep my business intact. I would end up selling the three ounces later that week.

JOYRIDE

Dominic and I were drawn together because we both had single mothers who worked long hours, and therefore we were less supervised than most kids.

One day we met up after school dressed in our usual wardrobe of baggy cargo shorts and sneakers. "Let's go to the mall," Dominic said, both hands stuffed inside his hoodie pockets.

"Let's go," I said.

Strolling to the mall, we talked about basketball, girls, and the latest sneakers that were about to be released. Dominic was telling me about some expensive Jordans that were destined to be a collector's items one day.

"My mom never gives me money for anything," I said. At that point I had built up a long list of resentments against her.

Being poor was just one of them. I thought having fresh sneakers was the most important thing in the world. Mom just didn't get it.

"How about your dad?" he asked.

"Nah, I don't really see him that much." I failed to mention that my dad was probably somewhere shacked up with a younger woman or using drugs. He would stop by once in a while, but he always looked skinnier than the time before. I hated him for being useless, but I had the most contempt for my mother, because she was the one who thought I should be grateful for a pair of Payless shoes. It was her fault that my life was a constant struggle, or so I thought.

"You want to hit the parking lot first?" Dominic asked.

"Yeah, man. Let's do it."

Recently, Dominic and I discovered that Toyota Camrys from the eighties could easily be broken into with just a half a pair of scissors. For the last few months, we had gotten items such as CDs, cameras, and computers out of cars, but we were always hoping that we'd find a wallet full of cash.

The Santa Monica mall had three stories with an adjacent parking lot. With a lack of security, we could easily walk down the aisles, acting like we had lost our car. With his facial hair, Dominic looked old enough to drive.

"No Camry in here," Dominic said.

"Let's go up toward Wilshire."

Dominic and I scanned the neighborhood on foot. It was hot, and I was tired of walking everywhere. Many kids at my school had gotten cars. We were on Arizona Avenue by an old folks home when I saw the sun shining down like a spotlight on a faded gray Camry.

"Would you look at that?" Dominic gave a nod.

"Finally."

"I'll keep a lookout," he said.

Within a few seconds, I was inside. But this time instead of ransacking the car, I shoved the scissors into the ignition. I was surprised when the engine turned over. I had already learned to drive in some of my friends' cars, so I looked up at Dominic, who was standing just outside the car. His eyes seemed to ask, "What should we do?" In an instant I had to decide whether to hop out or to take this baby for a ride. I never thought about any consequences. I just smiled and the decision was made. He hopped in and we drove off.

"Let's go to my house first," Dominic said.

"Good idea." We needed to figure out what we were going to do with the newly acquired car.

With my heart racing, a thin layer of sweat covered my forehead. I turned left down Fourth Street, and few minutes later we pulled up to Dominic's two-story fourplex. The bottom right unit had been vacant, and I can't remember how, but Dominic had a set of keys. It was our official hangout, and we pretended that the unit was our own apartment. It had dusty, unfinished hardwood floors, and we had furnished it with patio furniture that we had taken from the neighborhood. Once inside, my adrenaline was still pumping. "We just stole a car!" I said, slapping my forehead. I was shocked that I could do something so brazenly illegal and get away with it.

"That was so crazy, Rikki."

Dominic lit up a blunt to celebrate. We passed it back and forth while listening to Notorious B.I.G thump from the stereo and chilling on our stolen patio furniture. Once again, I had proven to myself that if you wanted something badly enough, you just had to go out there and get it.

***

One day after riding around town in the stolen car with Dominic and our friend Terrance, we picked up his cousin Q. He was older than us, with a dark complexion and a muscular build, and he played wide receiver at school. "Let me drive," he said, standing by the door.

"Sure. All right." I instantly surrendered the wheel. Who was I to argue with a senior who was bigger than me?

We drove around town with 92.3, the Beat, a local radio station, blasting from the speakers. Someone sparked up the weed, and all the windows went up to create a hot box so that we'd get even more high. We had been driving without any real destination for a while when Dominic said, "Let's go to Fox Hills Mall." Everyone was game.

When we walked into the indoor mall, the smells from the food court hit us first. "I need something to eat," I said. The weed had given me the munchies, and the junk food was calling my name.

After we got something to eat, we found a table. None of us talked while we ate. My friends slurped down sodas, pizza, and burgers while I had a sugary Cinnabon. By the time we came up for air, there was nothing left but empty paper wrappers and napkins crumpled on the table.

"Let's go to Foot Locker," Dominic said.

"Yo, that's my favorite store!" I replied.

As we passed by the window displays, we all gazed at the faceless, posed mannequins inviting us to come inside to try on the latest styles—camouflaged cargo jeans, bright T-shirts, matching hoodies, fitted hats, and aviator jackets, none of which I was able to afford.

We all stopped to stare when a hot girl in tight acid-washed jeans and pointy manicured nails walked by. I sighed as a warmth rippled up the back of my neck. Females hypnotized me. And none of us young men could take our eyes away from a swaying butt.

"Man, she looks goooood," Q said.

"She sure does." We all agreed.

Moments later we followed the sound of the loud hip-hop music coming from Foot Locker like it was the pied piper himself. Once inside the brightly lit store with all its neatly organized rows of sneakers, I felt internally embraced by that new shoe smell. From across the room, my eyes instantly lasered in on a pair of black-and-white Jordan 12s. It was love at first sight. When I got close enough, I ran my fingers across the smooth leather. *What I wouldn't do for a pair of sneakers like these.*

***

After we left the mall and were driving back to the club, Q whispered in a panic, "Oh shit! The cops."

My heart took off like a racehorse let out of the gate. "Oh fuck. Get rid of the weed," someone said.

Dominic threw out the weed just before multiple squad cars boxed us in. Guns drawn, dozens of cops approached us. I couldn't help but think back to the night I woke up surrounded by all those sheriffs. But this time, it was *me* they were after and not my mom.

"Hands in the air!" one cop yelled.

Everyone's hands shot up. One by one they ordered us to exit the car. My eyes darted around, looking for any form of escape, but it was pointless, and besides, I didn't want to get shot. Q was ordered out of the car first, and once they had him cuffed and in a patrol car, they'd have someone else get out. I was the last one to exit the car because I was in the back seat.

The cop barked out commands in rapid succession. "Hands up. Slowly. Back up to the sound of my voice. Interlock your fingers behind your head." Finally, I heard him holster his gun followed by the sound of the handcuffs clicking as he tightened them around my wrist. Then he led me to his squad car, where he reached inside my pockets and pulled out my wallet and a pack of Now and Laters and placed them on the hood. Once he was sure I didn't have any weapons or drugs, he placed his hand on top of my head and lowered me into the back seat of his car before slamming the door. My shoulders slouched in shame, I was convinced my entire family had to be cursed.

MENTOR

I was still hanging out with Gary Drake every weekend, but now I was on probation. He had asked Mom if I could go on a day trip with him and some of his AA friends to Buena Vista Lake in Kern County.

Mom gave her permission. Gary picked me up early on a Saturday morning for the two-hour drive. "So what's going on with you?" he asked.

"What do you mean?"

"I heard you've been getting into trouble lately."

"My mom told you?"

"She's concerned about you, and honestly, so am I." He gave me a stern look. "You know if you need something, Rikki, all you have to do is ask. You don't have to steal shit."

I wouldn't have asked because in my mind, Gary already did way too much.

"I mean it, knucklehead. I don't want to see you making the same mistakes I did when I was a kid." Gary had spent years in group homes and drug programs growing up.

"All right, all right. Next time I'll ask you if I need something." I hated confrontation, especially with Gary, whom I respected more than anyone else in the world. I just wanted the conversation to be over.

When we arrived at the lake, the sun was beating down, and there was a slight breeze. Some of the visitors were already backing up their boats onto the water. There was a grassy picnic area with food and drink set up. Gary introduced me to his friends. They were all really nice. After shoving a doughnut in my mouth, Gary placed a hand on my shoulder. "You ready to water ski, buddy?"

"I don't know. Is it hard?"

"You can do it. Besides, I'll walk you through it."

The captain of the boat, Gary's friend, had us put on orange life jackets. When we were ready, he said, "Here we go, everyone. Have a seat." The engine hummed as we traveled farther out onto the lake. When we got to the middle, Gary told me to jump in.

I swung my legs over the edge and dropped into the cool water, but the jacket made me bounce right back up.

"Put these on." Gary handed me two skis from the side of the boat. I slipped on the black neoprene footsies that were attached to the middle of the skis. I leaned back, and the tips of the skis poked out in front of me like a picket fence. The water sparkled, and gentle waves lapped at my face.

"Now what do I do?" I asked.

Gary tossed a rope, and it landed in front of my face. "Let the boat pull you up, but keep your knees bent," he said.

The engine roared, and the boat took off. I let the rope pull me, but when I crashed into the water on my side, I felt embarrassed. The boat circled me. Again, I tried standing. Again, I fell. It looked so easy when others did it. I felt stupid. Humiliated. I might have given up were it not for Gary's encouragement. "You got this, Rikki!" he yelled over the hum of the motor. "Remember to keep your knees bent."

The engine sputtered and then roared to life again. I took a deep breath and leaned back against the tension of the rope.

Gripping the handle, my arms extended and my thigh muscles tightened, I came up to a standing position. Suddenly the water was moving past me, and the wind was sweeping over my face. Gliding over ripples of frothy whitecaps as the boat soared around the edge of the lake, I felt so alive. When I hit a slightly larger wake, I lifted up, and for a brief moment, I was suspended in the air. It felt like I was flying.

I did three more loops of the lake, until eventually my thighs trembled with exhaustion. I let go of the rope and sank into the water. The adrenaline pumping through my bloodstream was the same feeling I got running from security guards after stealing shit. However, this had a much more positive outcome.

GAME TIME

During my sophomore year of high school, Mom and I were still living in transitional housing, my brother was locked up, and it looked like I might be headed down the same path. I was smoking weed, stealing, and failing many of my classes. The only things I was passionate about were basketball and girls. The basketball court gave me a place to release pent-up energy, frustrations, and disappointments.

One day C. C., an old friend from junior high, suggested that we go out for the school team. "They're having tryouts next Friday," he said.

"My grades are terrible. They won't let me play."

"Dude, they don't even check," he said.

"I guess it wouldn't hurt to try." Deep down I had dreams of playing high school basketball.

I played every day leading up to tryouts. I must have thrown a thousand shots by the time it rolled around.

When school let out on Friday, C. C. and I met at the gym. I was a wearing a pair of basketball shoes that I had borrowed from him because I didn't like the pair I had at the time.

I approached the assistant coach with a basketball tucked under my arm. He handed me a clipboard. "Sign up, then wait for the coach to call your name," he said.

The smell of competition and sweat hung in the air. The sound of screeching sneakers, whistles, and the coach's voice bounced off the walls. C. C. and I sat on the sidelines watching some of the school's best athletes perform. For a brief moment, I wondered what I was doing there. Then I told myself that I was good enough to play. Twenty minutes later the coach yelled my name.

"You got this," C. C. said as I joined the team.

The coach pointed and said, "Let's see what you can do."

The tryout consisted of shooting and dribbling drills, some five on five, and of course a lot of running. The coach yelled a series of continuous commands: "Shoot the ball!" "Get down there!" "Box out!" Four other coaches stood on the sidelines studying everyone's moves.

I excelled most during the five on five. I felt like there was no one on the court who could guard me. I was too quick. My right foot shifted back and forth when I faked a three and blew right by the defender before laying the ball up in the hoop. Tryouts took over four hours. I headed home feeling exhausted but confident that I had given it everything I had.

***

A week later, the list was posted in the gym. I squeezed sideways between guys to get a closer look. My heart sank when I didn't see my name. I looked at another list and was relieved to see it there. I turned to C. C. "We made the sophomore team."

"That's a good start," he said.

"If we play well enough, maybe we'll make varsity next year."

Later that day, we met Coach Thompson for orientation. He was muscular, confident, and enthusiastic. I sat next to C. C. and the other players lined up in the bleachers.

"You guys going to work hard this season?" Thompson asked.

"Yes, sir," everyone said in unison.

"I need you here every day for practice."

"Yes, sir."

Coach Thompson passed the burnt orange ball back and forth between his hands as he paced in front of us. Then he stopped and looked directly into our eyes, one at a time. He had such an intensity that you couldn't help but listen. "I want you to learn two things here." He held up his fingers in a peace sign. "Effort and execution. During any game you have to outplay the other team on every single possession. Run the floor as fast as you can." He pointed to the court. "And from an execution standpoint, you have to take care of the ball. That means you make the right play, not the one that makes you look good. Every offensive possession has to be about making the best possible decision, even if that means giving the ball away so someone else can make the shot."

I had never cared about history, geography, or math. I had never been coachable in a classroom setting, but I was certainly coachable when it came to the game. I thought that if I could learn how to shoot a three-pointer or knock down a midrange jump shot, then maybe some scout would see me, and I'd be recruited to play college ball. And who knows, maybe one day the NBA would come calling. So with a laser-like focus, I listened to everything the coach had to say.

That season, Coach Thompson's commitment to the team would pay off. Not only did we win some games but also he taught me how to perfect my offensive footwork, how to position myself to grab more rebounds, and how to be a team player. Determined to bring my best to the game, I stopped smoking weed and started doing my homework in order to bring up my grades. I was determined to give it all I had because playing ball was the only plan I had for my future. In my mind, it was my only way out.

GIRL TROUBLE

Santa Monica High School had a series of two-story buildings scattered around the campus, a network of hallways, and a newly installed gym. The breaks were chaotic, with bells ringing, sneakers squeaking, lockers slamming, and kids rushing to make it to class on time.

The first time I saw her was at quad during lunch break. She was a cute little Latina girl with a heart-shaped mouth. I wasn't sure if she was looking at me or over my head, but I was determined to find out. "Hey there," I said, walking up to her. "What's your name?"

"Jackie." She smiled, and two perfect dimples appeared in her cheeks as she gripped the strap on her backpack.

We made small talk. I could tell she was into me by the way

her one shoulder curled up to her ear.

"You want to come to my basketball game tomorrow at four?" I figured if I could get her to come, she would be impressed with how well I played.

"I'd like that."

"I'll look for you in the bleachers."

My heart pounded all the way to my next class. Girls had started to take up a lot of space in my mind. While I lacked experience, I had learned from my friends that acting confident could take you far.

The next day, Jackie sat in the bleachers with her silky black hair framing her face. Gary Drake and Mom were there too, but it was the sexy girl who made me play even harder. During warm-ups I flashed her a quick smile. From then on, Jackie and I hung out almost every day. I'd take her to my house before Mom got home from work. We'd make out, and I'd explore every curve of her body. We didn't have sex at first, but that changed after a week.

We'd been together for about three months when I started to notice that she wanted to be around me all the time. One day when I was hanging out with C. C., Jackie kept paging me.

"I don't know what to do about Jackie anymore," I said.

"Tell her you need some space, dude," C. C. said.

"I have, but she doesn't get it."

I had no experience with navigating relationships, and I certainly didn't know how to break up with someone. I'd finally had enough when Jackie started drilling me with questions like "Where have you been?" "Why are you ignoring me?" and "Why aren't we hanging out as much?"

"I can't do this anymore," I said on the phone.

"But you can't break up with me. We have something special."

"I don't want to see you again."

I felt bad when she started crying, but I was tired of her neediness. While I was ready to move on, Jackie wasn't about to let go. In fact, she called all the time. She'd follow me home after school, and even though I told her to leave me alone, she wouldn't listen.

Two weeks later I had a new interest in Sylvia, a light-skinned girl with dark curly hair. Sylvia and I had started talking on the phone, and we made plans to go out with a group of friends after my Friday night game.

When Friday rolled around, I was pumped up for the game. Sylvia and my friends were all in the stands, cheering for the team. Halfway through the game, Jackie came stomping in and plopped herself down on one of the bleachers. It was hard to concentrate with two girls in the stands watching me, but we still won the game. Afterward, I ignored Jackie and told my friends I'd see them later. The plan was for Sylvia to pick me up at home after I had showered.

Mom was at one of her recovery meetings. I had just gotten out of the shower when I heard a knock. When I opened the door, it was Jackie.

"I want to talk to you," she said.

"You need to stop coming over like this."

"But I miss you."

"I'm going out with my friends."

I don't remember what else we said, but after fifteen minutes of arguing, she headed for the bus stop. Not long after, Sylvia called to say she was in the back parking lot. I ran down the stairs and saw Jackie with a wild look in her eyes, holding a brick in her hand.

"Jackie, stop!" I yelled.

But it was too late. The brick went flying through the air and crashed against the bumper of Sylvia's Honda Accord. Jackie pointed at the car and screamed, "Who the fuck is that?"

I glanced at Sylvia, who was throwing the car in reverse. "None of your fucking business. Now get out of here."

"I hate you!" Jackie yelled. Then she ran toward me, her nails reaching for my face. *Oh my God! This girl has gone completely crazy.* I had to stop her, so I grabbed her in a bear hug and lowered her to the ground. Someone must have called the police, because a few minutes later, a squad car pulled up with two officers. They quickly separated us. I told them my side of the story, and Sylvia confirmed it. Jackie was put in the back of the squad car.

"Do you want to file a complaint?" one of the officers asked.

"No, that's all right."

"We're going to take her home," he said.

Sadly, I spent the night apologizing to Sylvia for the dent in her bumper. Most girls don't want to deal with guys who had crazy ex-girlfriends.

***

Two weeks after that disastrous night, I was in my room when Mom called out, "Rikki? Jackie is here to see you."

I rolled off my mattress, pulled on a T-shirt, and walked into the living room. Jackie was standing there looking sad. "I want to talk to you," she said.

Although Mom knew we had broken up, I hadn't told her why. "Let's go outside." I stormed out the door and down the steps. "You can't just pop in here whenever you want."

"I'm pregnant."

"What?" My breath caught in my throat.

"I'm going to have your baby."

"How do you know?"

"I did a home pregnancy test."

My mind searched for the right thing to say or do. I couldn't imagine being a father so young. The rest of the conversation was a blur, but she had clearly gotten my attention. I rarely confided in my mother except when I didn't know what to do. And this was one of those rare occasions. I went back upstairs, sat down next to Mom, and told her everything: how Jackie had been stalking me, how she wouldn't leave me alone, and how she'd thrown a brick at Sylvia's car.

"That sounds like something I might do," Mom said, smiling.

"Mom, stop it!" I thought she wasn't taking me seriously enough. "And now she claims she's pregnant."

Mom's hand shot straight up to her mouth. "What? You had sex?" She narrowed her eyes.

"Yes, we did." All my friends had done it before, but none of them had been forced to tell their mothers about it. It was humiliating. But what choice did I have? "But I think she's lying," I added.

Mom inhaled deeply. "We need to find out, Rikki."

"But how?"

"Tell her I'll take her to the family planning clinic for a test."

"What if she doesn't want to go?"

"Then she's probably lying to keep you around."

"That's crazy," I said.

The next day, I told Jackie over the phone that we needed to go to the family clinic, but she said she couldn't go. It felt like my entire future could be determined by those test results. I kept calling her about taking the test, but she continued making excuses. I was left in a constant state of anxiety. I kept thinking that if I was a father, I'd have to get a job to support her. I'd have to give up on all my dreams of playing basketball. I'd have to learn how to be a dad.

A month after she dropped the bombshell, she called me. "I had a miscarriage," she said.

"What?"

"I lost the baby."

I let out an exasperated sigh. I knew it had all been a hoax. "Don't ever call me again, Jackie." I hung up. After that, if I saw her on campus, I went the other way.

***

My first attempt at a serious relationship had ended up being nothing but lies, violence, and a girl in the back of a police car. All of which pretty much mirrored Mom's behavior with Dad before she got sober. While Mom had been out of jail for six years now and our lives had improved, we still struggled to make ends meet.

Although I may not have been conscious of it at the time, I started to associate all females with betrayal, pain, and drama. I started to think Mom and Jackie were merely cautionary tales, and without realizing it, I put up an invisible shield around my heart, determined not to let another girl in.

COUNSELOR VERSUS COACH

At seventeen, I was still playing basketball on the junior varsity team, but I started to fall behind in my grades again. I couldn't seem to muster the motivation anymore. One day after practice, Coach Thompson pulled me aside. "Rikki, let's grab a bite at McDonalds."

Although I found it a little odd that he asked just me, I figured he wanted to give me some coaching tips. Walking into McDonalds, I was hit with the familiar smell of ketchup, mustard, and grease with an underlying hint of disinfectant. We both ordered Big Mac combos and grabbed a table near the front. I was about to stuff my mouth with fries saturated in ketchup when Coach asked, "What's going on, Rikki?"

The fries stopped midair. "What do you mean?"

"Your grades."

"Oh, that. I'm having a hard time studying for some reason."

He leaned forward and looked me dead in the eye. "Don't you want to play basketball?"

"Yeah. More than anything else."

"You're a damn good player, Rikki, and the team needs you." He paused to let this land. "But I can't let you play if you're failing your classes."

My stomach tightened in a knot. I hated disappointing someone I looked up to, let alone disappointing myself. "I just can't seem to get my head around the math."

"What if I found a tutor for you?"

In my mind, it always circled back to not having money. Mom told me a thousand times in a thousand different ways that we couldn't afford the things other people had. She constantly complained about not having anything left over after she paid the bills. She complained about not being able to go to a nice restaurant. Not having enough to buy me a pair of Jordans. "My mom can't afford a tutor." I lowered my head.

"I might know someone who would volunteer his time."

What I didn't tell the coach was that while I wanted to play ball, I didn't want to learn algebra. It was a stupid subject and one that I was convinced I'd never have any use for, but if that's what it took, I was willing to spend an hour each week learning it. "That would be great."

When the coach drove me home, the sky was turning several shades of burnt orange. "I want to talk to your mom, so I'll go up with you," he said.

My gut clenched. I hadn't expected that. Our one-bedroom apartment was filled with used furniture. I was grateful that we had our own place, but I wondered if Coach Thompson would find out my secret of being in transitional living.

We walked into a cloud of smoke from Mom's cigarette. She was home from work and had changed into her normal evening attire of sweatpants and an oversize T-shirt. Embarrassment made its way up the back of my neck.

"Oh, hi, Coach." She stubbed the butt into the ashtray and stood up. "Sorry, I wasn't expecting anybody."

"No worries. I just wanted to let you know Rikki and I had a little talk at McDonalds." He paused. "I think a math tutor might help him."

"Um, isn't that expensive?" A questioning eyebrow shot up.

"I think I have a student who'd be willing to volunteer."

"Oh really? I'm certainly not good at math so that would be great."

"He needs to bring his grades up if he wants to play ball."

Mom looked at me. "You hear that, Rikki? If you want to keep playing—"

"Yes, Mom." My jaw tightened. Another reason I didn't want anyone to come over was because Mom was liable to say something embarrassing.

"Well, it's settled then. I'll make it happen," Coach said.

After he left, Mom said, "That was nice of Coach Thompson. He must care about you a lot to want to get you help."

She often tried to engage me in conversation, but I usually just pushed her away. "Yeah, Mom."

"Not everyone who works at that school cares about the kids," she said before I retreated to my room.

***

Almost to prove Mom's point, a week later we were called into the counselor's office.

"Thank you for coming, Mrs. Adamson. Have a seat."

We sat in the hard chairs on the other side of his desk. "Yeah. Well, I had to call my work and tell them I'd be late."

"I appreciate that." He looked at me. "Hey, Rikki. How's it going?"

"It's going good." I knew this was his attempt to butter me up before he dropped the axe.

He picked up a manila folder. "I wanted to talk to you about your grades. You're falling behind again."

"Coach Thompson just got me a tutor for math."

"I'm glad to hear that, but you'll need to work on more than just your math. You have bad grades in English, geography, and history."

I gazed at the floor.

He leaned forward with an I'm-really-concerned about-your-future look. "Do you have any plans for what you want to do after high school?"

"I want to play basketball."

An all-knowing grin spread over his face. He nodded. "Well, Rikki, a lot of kids want to play ball, and I'll tell you what I tell them: You need to focus on a more realistic goal. Very few kids go on to play professional ball."

My face turned hot. "But that's my dream."

I don't remember what else was said, but later Mom told me she saw how crushed I was by his words. "I don't know why a school counselor would tell you that," she said. "He could have suggested college ball or coaching. Anything but slamming down your dream."

"Maybe he's right." My self-doubt was so close to the surface, and it didn't take much for me to question myself. After that day, what little motivation I had was gone.

I didn't realize it at the time, but while there were plenty of people like Coach Thompson, Gary Drake, and even my mom trying their best to build me up, all it took was one burned-out school counselor to knock me down.

RELOCATE

During my senior year, and after five years of transitional living, we finally moved into an apartment complex in Culver City. Once again, my mother gave me the bedroom while she made the dining room into her bedroom. Although it was a small unit and thirty minutes from school, I liked the fact that I would be able to invite my friends over to swim in the pool.

A week after moving, I was called into the school counselor's office. I assumed it was once again because of my grades, but he had other news.

"I'm sorry, Rikki, but since you're not living in the Santa Monica school district, you will have to transfer to Hamilton High," he said.

"What? Can't I just finish my senior year here?"

"I'm afraid not."

I knew he was looking for a reason to get rid of me because he considered me a troublemaker, but I didn't want to leave all my friends and have to start over again.

"We'll send your transcripts over to Hamilton." He stood up and extended his hand. "Best of luck to you, Rikki."

I was speechless as I turned and walked away.

Later, when I told Mom what had happened, she was pissed. "They could have at least let you finish out the year," she said.

"I don't want to go to a new school where I don't know anyone."

"I know, Rikki, but you're almost done."

The following Monday, Mom went with me to Hamilton High, a multicolored brick building closer to where we were now living. I felt pangs of nervousness about starting a new school. There weren't any friends to greet me like there would have been at my old school. Mom asked the security guard where the admissions office was. Once inside, we were surrounded by loud kids who all seemed to know each other. Some were racing down the corridor, others were putting backpacks into their lockers, and some were just talking to their friends. They didn't look at me. As a new kid, I was invisible to them.

Mom signed the enrollment paperwork, and after I got my class schedule, she left for work. The day dragged on as I was weighed down with self-consciousness. I ate lunch alone. I walked the hallways alone. I sat alone.

During my last period of the day, two cops in dark-blue uniforms came strutting into the classroom and headed for the teacher. They spoke in whispered tones, and although I couldn't hear what they were saying, I knew exactly why they were there.

***

A few days earlier, I had been hanging out with Dominic, Elijah, and Ben at the hideout—the empty apartment that Dominic still had keys to.

"Why don't we go get some clothes from Unlimited?" Dominic said. We had all shoplifted there separately, but going in as a group and grabbing jackets and designer jeans was a new idea.

"So what are you thinking?" I asked.

"We'll grab everything we can near the exit and run out at the same time."

With everyone on board, we pulled up to the adjacent alley

behind Unlimited. Three of us climbed out while Ben kept his blue Impala running. Once inside, things happened really fast. All of us scooped up dozens of jeans and jackets and rushed out the door. With our arms filled with merchandise, pedestrians glared at us. I could hear my heart beating inside my head once everyone was back in the car. "What do we do now?" Ben asked.

"We should get out of Santa Monica and go over to my house," I said.

"The hideout is closer," Dominic said.

Making a right turn, Ben drove toward the hideout when a police car passed us. "Don't look at them. Don't look at them," I repeated. But it was too late. The cops did one of those screeching, rubber-burning U-turns, and we all knew what was coming next. There were a few muttered comments of "Oh fuck" and "Shit" before the siren yelped behind us like a dog in pain.

"I'm not getting into some high-speed chase," Ben said, pulling the car over to the curb.

My heart felt like it might jump clear out of my throat. I knew immediately that I needed to get out of there, so I pushed the clothes off my lap and flung the side door open. Someone yelled from behind for me to stop, but I wasn't about to break my stride. I sprinted through an apartment complex to the back alley, my arms and legs pumping furiously. I ran faster than I ever had on any basketball court, that's for sure, and within ten minutes, I was back at the hideout.

I flinched when Elijah came rushing in behind me. He bent over and placed his hands on his knees. "I think they might have gotten Dominic," he said.

Still out of breath, I peeked out the mini blinds and watched cop cars race up Fourth Street looking for us.

"I told you we should have left Santa Monica."

"It's too late now," Elijah said.

"Well, I'm getting out of here." I had basketball shorts on under my cargo pants, so I took a layer off. "I'll call you later," I said, heading out the front door.

My plan was to go to Lincoln Park, where I often played basketball. Once I got there, my hands were shaking as I started to shoot around with another kid. I felt safe on the court. What cop was going to look for a kid shooting hoops? Later I took the bus home, and the next day I finally got ahold of Dominic. "Hey, man. What happened to you?"

"I hid in a dumpster until the cops found me."

"What happened then?"

"I have to go to court for theft."

"What happened to Ben?"

"I don't know. They separated us when we got to the station."

Now, standing in front of my new classmates in handcuffs, I was humiliated. Later, when Mom came to pick me up at the Santa Monica police station, she was livid and went off on me.

I was grounded for the next two weeks, but Mom let me see Gary, who had been hanging out with me every weekend for over seven years. To Mom, Gary was the one and only consistent male figure in my life. When he picked me up, he asked, "What the hell is going on with you?"

Without any reasonable excuse, I shrugged.

"You know, it's real easy going down the path you're on, fuckhead. Your dad went down it, your mom went down it, and so did I. And if that's the path you chose to take, I want you to know I'll always love you and I'll even come visit you when they lock your ass up, but I really hope you don't go down that path."

I crossed my arms over my chest and didn't say a thing. Although Gary may have thought I wasn't listening, I heard every word.

At court, we were all given probation and community ser-
vice. Although I would never get arrested again, I still couldn't
turn my life around. I needed money, and going to school was
getting in the way of that, so I dropped out and started taking
random jobs that paid minimum wage. But the money was never enough to fix me. I lived in a constant state of deprivation,
and no matter what I earned, I always wanted more.

OH BROTHER

By 2003, my brother, Jerry, already had three kids: four-year-old Alyssa, who lived with his ex-girlfriend; two-year-old Mariah; and newborn Marc, who he had with his wife, Erika. The fear of missing out on his kids' lives had motivated Jerry to get a job and find a home.

I was twenty years old when Jerry called to ask if I wanted to play on a basketball league. I was still in love with the game, so of course I said yes. Every week Jerry and I would meet in our old neighborhood to practice or play a game with his best friend, Marc. Jerry had been out of prison for nearly two years but was still muscular from all the weight lifting he did while in there. But he was agile on the court, and our timing was impeccable. I knew just when to pass the ball to him. After we won a game at Lomita Park, Jerry wiped sweat from his forehead with a small towel.

"Hey, bro," he said. "You should rent my downstairs unit." He had a two-story apartment in Hawthorne. Living with Mom was cheap, but I was ready to get out on my own.

"You can have girls over whenever you want," he said.

The following weekend, I arrived at his place and met his son, Marc, named after his best friend Marc from the park. He was just a few months old and bundled up in a blanket inside his crib. I looked down at his pink cherub mouth and long lashes. "Oh my God. He's so cute," I said.

"He's perfect." Jerry beamed. "Doesn't it make you want to have one of your own?"

"Nope. That's not for me."

"What the hell are you talking about? Kids will change your life."

"I'm not looking for that kind of responsibility," I said. "Besides, I can't see myself settling down with one girl."

"That's because you haven't found the right one yet." Jerry claimed Erika was the love of his life and had motivated him to straighten out.

We did a quick walk-through of the kitchen, the bathroom, and the master bedroom before heading downstairs. The unit had low ceilings. It was dark and compressed, but at the time, I just wanted to be on my own, so it would work.

"You have your very own entrance." Jerry opened the door, and on the other side was a reinforced iron gate. "And a little extra security so you can sleep better at night." Gripping the bar, he rattled it to demonstrate its strength. "What do you think?" he asked.

I smiled. "When can I move in?"

Later, Mom was surprised when I told her. "But why do you want to leave?" she asked. "You only have to pay a hundred dollars living here."

I shrugged. "I think it's about time I get my own place."

The following weekend I moved my queen bed, a dresser, and a nightstand and started decorating my new bachelor pad. Cool lighting and a stereo to play my favorite music. With a steady job at Gary Drake's construction company, I had been able to finance a black Toyota Solara. So not only was my rent higher but also I had a car payment and insurance to pay every month. Since I never learned how to balance a budget, I was often late on my car payments.

But being on my own felt great. I could party as much as I wanted and have random girls come over after the clubs closed. I didn't remember their names or even what they looked like. I remember meeting one girl while I was cruising Sunset Boulevard on a Friday night. Another girl drove her mother's red Mercedes and then there was the pretty model who always flaunted her cleavage. I slept with all of them, but it was always just another mouth, another ass, or another set of calf muscles stiff and ropey around my back. Having sex was another way for me to attain a glimmer of relief. As long as I distracted myself with something, it worked to keep an undercurrent of sadness at bay.

I had been at my brother's for about a year when, one night, two guys were fighting outside my window and one of them got body-slammed on top of my car. It broke my windshield, and I had to pay $300 to get it fixed. Right after that, it got repossessed because I hadn't made the payments on time.

After that I started hating everything about my life. I hated digging ditches at the construction site. I felt out of place with all the Mexican laborers who spoke Spanish. I hated where I was living. The depression reminded me of when I was getting in trouble as a teenager and Mom forced me to see a therapist. I would sit in her office, arms crossed over my chest, refusing to say a word the entire hour. The therapist seemed like she cared and would try different methods to get me to open up. But I was determined not to let anyone in and armored up. Eventually, the therapist told Mom that she wasn't getting anywhere with me, so I stopped going to the sessions. Now the sadness was creeping back in.

One day Mom gave me the number of a guesthouse for rent. After making an appointment with Bill, the landlord, I drove up a steep hill on a private road off Jefferson Boulevard. Bill worked in the movie industry and showed me around his compound. The first thing I noticed was the breathtaking view of the city, followed by the swimming pool and a Jacuzzi next to the light-yellow guesthouse with brown trim. When we entered the space, light streamed through the windows, making it seem much bigger than it was.

"I would love to live here," I said.

"I have one more person looking at it, so I'll give you a call when I make up my mind."

Bill called me the following week and told me I could have the place. I moved in right away, and it felt like things were finally looking up.

PARTY HARD

December 30, 2006

Jake and I had met back in my senior year at Hamilton High. He was tall, good looking, and always drove flashy cars. For some reason we had bonded, and now five years later, it was Jake's twenty-fourth birthday. He had gone to great lengths to plan a special night, and I was ready to celebrate in my burgundy and white Air Force 1s, a matching Ralph Lauren long-sleeve shirt, and $300 designer jeans. My outfit probably cost more than my entire Costco paycheck, where I was working at the time, and while I hated the job, it provided money to buy fresh sneakers, which was high on my list of priorities.

When Jake answered the door, he was wearing black Nike high-top Dunks that sold for over $1,300. "Yo, Rikki. What's good?" He stepped aside to let me in.

"Yo, happy birthday! You excited for tonight?" I asked.

"Yeah, man. I have a few friends coming over for drinks, and a limo will pick us up around eleven to take us to the club."

"Oh, a limo? That sounds perfect," I said.

Jake's parents had helped him buy a condo. The living room alone was four times the size of my guesthouse. I sat down on the couch as Jake poured us shot glasses filled with Patrón. I wasn't a big drinker because I had seen the havoc it had wreaked on my family; however, I understood the attraction because anytime alcohol hit my bloodstream, it could make music more enjoyable and girls suddenly more attractive. As I threw back the shot, the warmth of the tequila crept down my throat and spread across my chest. Instantly, a calm washed over me.

"Hey, can I turn on the PlayStation?" I asked.

"Yeah, go for it."

Jake and I could spend hours playing *Call of Duty* online. We were completely addicted to that game.

Eventually the doorbell rang, and even though I didn't want to, I stopped playing. There were eight of us sitting in the living room doing shots and laughing. Jake's girlfriend, Destiny, was there as well as James, the club promoter, and his girlfriend.

The limo pulled up at 11:00 p.m. It had cost Jake a few hundred dollars, and we only had to drive three and a half miles. Arriving at the White Lotus, one of Hollywood's best spots at the time, a long line of twentysomethings circled around the block. The politics of Hollywood nightlife dictated that the girls showing the most skin would be let in first while the guys would be pushed to the back. When we hopped out of the limo, all eyes were on us.

Glancing down the line, I saw people I knew, so I tried to avoid direct eye contact. I didn't want to feel pressured to get them in. There was something special about skipping the line. Since we were with the event promoter, the velvet rope was lifted up for us. I could imagine all the girls saying, "Wait, who are those guys?" A moment of celebrity could increase the odds of going home with a random girl.

The club was packed. "Good Life" by Kanye West was thumping through the speakers as a DJ hyped up the crowd. It felt like we were moving in slow motion as we were escorted to our table.

Three waitresses wearing fishnet stockings and booty shorts arrived with top-shelf bottles of liquor. "Anyone down for some

Gray Goose?" Before we could even sit, Jake was filling everyone's glass. I sipped on my vodka and OJ. The DJ was on an elevated platform with purple and yellow lights flashing around him. I wondered if he was a Lakers fan. The drug dealers were off in the corner. They had a steady line of people stopping by to say hello. The gangbangers had a few tables near the secondary bar. That section was off limits. I focused on the pretty girls in the middle of the dance floor. I was hopeful that I could catch at least one of them walking off and possibly get her number. The night was moving quickly, and I knew that with each passing moment, I had less of a chance to meet a beautiful stranger. So like a quarterback calling an audible, I changed the play. I had another drink and took one more lap around the club. I made eye contact with a pretty girl. She held my stare for a good five seconds. I walked over and positioned myself behind her. "Hey, I'm Rikki. Can I get your number?"

"No," she said and walked off.

Defeated, I headed back to the table. When I got there, one of the girls I had come with was crying. "What's going on?" I asked.

"The bouncers just threw my boyfriend out!"

"What? Why?"

"James fell off the couch. They said he was too drunk."

I felt like our best move would be to escort the girls to the front door.

As soon as we stepped outside, it was chaos. Jake and James were both yelling and pushing the bouncers. Two of the largest bouncers started throwing punches and choking out Jake. I jumped in swinging. These motherfuckers were the size of linebackers, and they focused solely on me. Instantly, I realized my mistake. They chased me into the middle of the street.

With my fists up in a defensive stance, I saw a shorter Hispanic bouncer in my peripheral vision. He hit me on the side of the head so hard that I was knocked out before I hit the ground. I don't know how long I was out, but when I came to, I was missing my front tooth. The same one I had lost in high school playing basketball. Blood was pouring down my face from a gash in my forehead. I pushed myself up and slowly made my way to the parking structure across the street. I didn't see any of my friends, so I called my mom. It was 1:00 a.m.

"Mom, I have to go to the hospital." It was surprising how calm I was.

"Oh no. What happened?"

"I got jumped."

"I'll be right there," she said.

After hanging up, I looked down at my Air Forces. Blood blended with the burgundy patent leather.

Jake eventually found me wandering in the parking garage. "Come on, dude. Let's go," he said.

I hopped into the limo. I heard someone say that it was going to be expensive to clean the blood off the floor. "Just take me to the ER!" I yelled. I was furious that they were more concerned about that dumbass limo than getting me some help. "Man, what the fuck happened?" I couldn't remember anything.

"After you got knocked out, two or three of them started kicking you in the head. I thought you were going to die, so I had to break it up," Ronnie said, who I had just met that night.

"Dude. What the fuck?" I was already thinking of ways to come back and shoot up the place.

In the emergency room, I took note of the fact that it was Destiny who stayed with me while Jake took off. A few minutes later, as I was being checked in, Mom rushed in with a look of horror all over her face. "I'm sorry, Mom."

"It's okay. It's okay," she said, rubbing my shoulder.

"I lost my tooth again."

"We'll get it fixed," Mom reassured me.

The physical scars of that night left me with twelve stitches on my forehead and needing a dental implant. But deeper than that were the emotional scars of trauma and the depression that settled on me like a black cloud. I spent weeks isolating in my guesthouse. I felt humiliated for getting jumped, and I was disappointed in my so-called friends. I hired an attorney to file a lawsuit. But as things moved forward, everyone who had been there flaked on me when it came to showing up as a witness in court. Although my attorney was able to settle for $10,00, it didn't make up for what I had endured. After that incident, I not only stopped hanging out with Jake but also I never drank again.

MOUNTAIN DEW

After three years of punching a clock at Costco, I was let go for being late and calling in too much. But truthfully I didn't care. At twenty-five, I was tired of dealing with entitled customers who treated me like shit. Tired of the coworkers trying to climb the corporate ladder. Tired of gathering shopping carts under a hot sun in the parking lot. If it wasn't for my obsession with sneakers, I might not have worked there for so long. At the time I had over a hundred pairs of sneakers in my collection, and I wanted more.

When I started looking for a new job, they always seemed to want to know the answers to the same questions: Do you have a high school diploma? Have you ever been arrested? As far as I was concerned, it was none of their damn business. After two months, desperation was setting in, so I signed up with a temporary employment agency. They found me a job in the financial district. It was four hours a day, four days a week, at minimum wage. My weekly gross income would be $120. That was pretty gross all right, but I had nothing else going for me.

It was in downtown Los Angeles, where I had to sort and file paperwork in alphabetical order and then archive it in a windowless basement. Just like school, the work seemed pointless, but I couldn't figure out what else to do with my life. I felt like such a fucking loser.

I had been working since I was seventeen but couldn't seem to find a steady job. One of my first jobs was at the Aquarium and Pet Center in Santa Monica. My friend C. C. from high school was the store manager, so he was able to get me in. Although we had to clean puppy shit and stock shelves, it was still fun working with a friend. At eighteen I started working at Toys R Us. The only thing I remember from that job is that the day after 9/11, my manager had us join in a moment of silence over the loudspeaker. I had also worked for Gary Drake's construction company, but doing manual labor never appealed to me.

Now I was filing paperwork in some financial building downtown. The only good thing about the job was that my supervisor let me listen to music on my iPod. I was carrying a box to the dumpster when I asked myself, *This is all I have to offer the world? There's got to be more than this.*

Right then DMX's song "The Convo" came on. Hearing the lyrics about how he'd gotten lost in life until he finally realized that God always had his back hit me hard. In that moment it felt as if DMX was talking directly to me. I started crying right there. I needed to do something, and it wasn't filing paperwork in the financial district.

I called Mom. "I can't take this job anymore. I'm going to quit."

"You can't leave one job without having another lined up."

Mom tried to talk me out of it, but it was pointless. Moments later I talked to my supervisor, who wished me the best of luck.

A week later I was jobless, depressed, and wondering if Mom had been right when she called me with an opportunity I never saw coming. "My friend Cathi is a casting director. I told her about you, and she said to have you come in for an audition at her office," she said.

"What? I'm not an actor."

"It doesn't matter, Rikki. Just show up."

It might have been the timing, but I was in such a desperate place that I said, "Fuck it. I'll give it a shot."

The day of the casting call, I got the script for the commercial. The scene was a suspicious guy being stopped and searched by the police. *Are you kidding? I have plenty of real-life experience getting jacked by the police.*

When I walked into Cathi's office, it was filled with good-looking professional actors. They were all focused on perfecting their lines. Many held yo-yos. "What are the yo-yos for?" I asked when I signed in.

"It's a prop for the audition. Think of the yo-yo as a weapon."

"I didn't know I had to bring my own yo-yo." My head began to spin. I had messed up already. *Why the fuck was I even here?*

Twenty minutes later, I was called into the screening room with two other actors. The room had soundproof walls, lights, and a camera. The camera operator gave us directions. "State your name and your age."

Watching the other actors perform their scenes, my heart fluttered with anxiety. I remembered how nervous I had been when I was pulled over by the police. I told myself to use that same nervous energy for the part. The camera operator played the role of the officer. "Where are you going?" he said.

"I'm on my way home."

"Then what is this?" He flipped an imaginary yo-yo in his hand. Improvising, I slammed my chest onto the six-foot table like it was a police car and yelled my line. "It's not mine! It's my cousin's yo-yo." The whole room cracked up. Even the actors. That was it. My first audition was over. I made sure to find Cathi before I left to thank her.

"Well, let's see if you get a callback," she said.

I had no idea how any of it worked, but a couple of days later, I did get a call saying they wanted me back for a second audition. I was shocked when I ended up booking a national Mountain Dew commercial, playing a guy getting stopped by the police. It all happened so fast, from crying about having to file paperwork to having my own trailer on a film set. I reflected back to the DMX song and thought maybe DMX was right. Maybe God had been carrying me all along.

CREATIVE OUTLET

After booking the Mountain Dew commercial, Mom told me about another opportunity. She knew a production manager who ended up getting me into production for commercials and music videos. The hours were long and the jobs were physically demanding, but being in a creative environment was far better than working in a Costco parking lot.

One of my first gigs was on a music video that took place in a vacant warehouse in downtown Los Angeles. Part of my responsibilities included setting up the video village with director's chairs, six-foot tables, and a trash can.

The artist performing that day was a rapper named Fabolous. Half a dozen beautiful female dancers in miniskirts and shorts were also in the video. They lined up behind Fabolous, then walked across the set striking seductive poses. I always carried a camera with me because I liked capturing cool moments. The lighting was perfect, and during each take I would snap away, capturing Fabolous and the women. When I showed my photos to the dancers, one of them said, "Can you send those to me?"

"Sure thing." Usually I was shy, but her feedback gave me enough confidence to approach the director, who always made sure his film crew was taken care of. "Hey, Jessy. I'd like to show you some photos I took."

"Sure," he said, looking at each picture slowly. "These are good. You should do this professionally."

"Wow. That means a lot to me," I said. He patted my shoulder and walked away.

While he might not remember that moment, his words were all it took to change the course of my life. From that point on, all I wanted to do was take photos. Instead of spending all my money on my sneaker collection, I started using some of my money to upgrade my camera. It took me a month of production assistant jobs before I was able to purchase my first Canon Rebel. I became enamored with the beauty of the world, capturing images of flowers and sunsets. I also took headshots of friends. I learned that every photographer has a niche, and I was lucky to have beautiful women who'd model for me.

As I started to build my portfolio, I posted my photographs on Instagram, a new social media outlet in 2010. It offered a cool place to profile your art; however, I soon discovered that everyone in the world wanted to be a photographer. It was discouraging to not get the likes and adoration I thought my photographs deserved. If I saw a photographer working on a film set, I only saw their success. I didn't see all the hard work they had put in to get there. The more I compared myself to others, the more I despaired. In the end, it always circled back to my belief that I wasn't good enough. In my mind, I had already failed.

ACT 3

PHOENIX

In 2014, I woke up around 4:00 a.m. with the ceiling fan spinning like a helicopter above my bed. I had been avoiding the pain all my life, but once again, I was in a dark place. Depression and despair weighed me down. At thirty-one, I had no real purpose in my life. It made me feel like the challenging things I had been through somehow got baked into my bones when I was a kid. I was afraid that the pain would never go away. It was a crushing blow when I finally realized that the problem I'd been running from all my life was me.

I had spent the last seven years working as a production assistant. I hated the long hours, the rude producers, and the meaninglessness of making advertising commercials.

I didn't have any work that day, so it would have been easy

to stay in bed. When I rolled over on my side, my gaze landed on the shoeboxes stacked against the wall. By that time, I had more than 150 pairs of sneakers in every color and style you could imagine. I had spent thousands of dollars in order to look good. And for what? So others would notice my dope sneakers whenever I walked into a room? Or so I wouldn't feel less than everybody else? In the end, I still hated myself.

In a moment of clarity, I sat up in bed. *What am I doing with so many shoes? I don't even wear most of them. There must people out there who could use them more than me. What if I gave some of my sneakers away? That's it. That's what I'm going to do.*

When I called my mom and told her about my idea, there was a slight pause on the other end of the phone. "Are you sure you want to give them away?" she asked.

"I've never been more sure of anything in my life."

"How do you plan on doing it?"

"I don't know yet, but I'll figure it out."

In a flash of inspiration, I knew that this new venture, whatever it would end up being, would be called Hav A Sole. That name seemed fitting, as it came from somewhere else.

Minutes later, I was pulling the shoeboxes down. Going through my collection was like taking a stroll down memory lane. I opened a box that held a pair of low-top Nike Dunks with a zebra print. I had bought them in 2004, and ten years later they still looked brand new. I moved around sorting and organizing, stacking and restacking the boxes until the sun was peeking through the blinds. I had thirty pairs of sneakers ready to give away. I cradled the boxes in my arms, then took them outside and stacked them on the deck. I took a photos of the shoes, posted them on Instagram, and wrote a caption: "I'm about to hit the streets and give my shoes away."

I loaded up the back of my Ford Explorer, and before I left, I grabbed a few warm hoodies that I didn't wear anymore.

Driving in an industrial area with nondescript buildings in Culver City, I saw a man sleeping on the sidewalk. I made a U-turn and parked across the street. I had no real plan as I approached him, but I knew I didn't want to scare him. "Good morning," I said. "What's your name?"

"My name is Phoenix."

"Hey, Phoenix. I'm Rikki. What size shoe do you wear?"

"I'm a size thirteen."

He was squinting up at me. It never occurred to me until then that not everyone was going to wear my shoe size. "Do you want a hoodie?"

"Yeah, man. That would be cool."

I rushed back to my car to retrieve the hoodie and gave it to Phoenix. He zipped it up. "Have a seat," he said, waving his hand.

The area was littered with fast-food wrappers, bottles, and empty beer cans. The smell of urine and alcohol hung in the air. I didn't want to sit on the dirty ground, but I figured that's what I had signed up for, so I sat next to him. When Phoenix gazed upward, I couldn't help but notice the thin layer of dirt that covered his neck and face like a second skin. It felt awkward, and I wondered if I should just leave.

Then he looked me and said, "Don't trust that girl."

I wasn't sure if he was talking about all girls in general or the one who had recently disappointed me, so I just laughed it off.

"How are things going with your father?" he asked.

That took me completely by surprise. It had been just two weeks since I visited Dad in the ICU, when we all thought he was going to die. "That's crazy you ask. He just got out of the hospital from a near overdose."

"Well, you need to call him right away."

"All right, I will." I didn't know what else to say.

Then Phoenix lifted his hands above his head and looked at the sky. He said, "Don't worry, I'm going to tell him exactly what he needs to hear." He looked back at me and asked, "What do you do for work?"

"Um, I'm a photographer."

"You need to put your work out there. Put it all over the internet."

"It's hard to stand out when everyone is trying to be a photographer these days."

"You *need* to put yourself out there." His tone was stern. "Look at me. This is all I have left in the world." His voice cracked as he dumped coins from a coffee cup onto the ground. "I am a computer expert. I can program computers, but no one will even give me a chance." He swept the coins closer to him with his dirty, cupped hands.

We talked for a good thirty minutes. Listening to Phoenix took me out of myself and gave me a different perspective. Hearing the struggles of another human being made my problems seem incredibly small. But it also felt like I had made a new friend.

Back in my car, I posted a photo of my shoes with a caption asking if anyone had a pair of size thirteens laying around. The thread blew up with comments like "I love what you're doing." "I have size nines in my closet you can have." "What a great idea. I can send you size elevens." And within a few minutes, Pierre, a good friend of mine, said he had some thirteens he didn't wear.

A week later, I went back to look for Phoenix. "Hey, Phoenix."

He tilted his head sideways. "Who are you?"

"What do you mean? I gave you the hoodie you're wearing."

He looked down as if seeing it for the first time. "Oh, this? I don't remember how I got it. Maybe I was in a blackout."

"Wow. That's crazy."

"All I remember is some shadowy figure with a smile standing over me," he said. "When I came to, I was wearing this. But you know what? I haven't had a drink since that day."

It was ironic that the conversation with Phoenix had such an impact on me, but he couldn't even remember it. Nonetheless, it would end up changing my life.

HAV A SOLE

I was all in with Hav A Sole. Giving out shoes to people resonated with me. Not only because I knew how important it was to have proper footwear but also because I knew people were suffering, and for the first time, I wanted to do something to help alleviate their pain. Moving fast, I secured a domain, a website, and all the social media handles. Friends and volunteers rallied to help me because I certainly didn't know what I was doing. My friend Marc designed a cool logo while I spoke to an attorney about getting our nonprofit status. I did all of this without any real business experience, pretty much figuring things out as I went along.

I continued using my Ford Explorer for direct outreach, looking for potential people to give out shoes to. One day I was going down a street not far from Skid Row when I saw a man asleep in an alcove in a bank. I did a quick U-turn and parked my car. I didn't want to scare him, but I saw that he didn't have shoes on at all. I approached slowly and whispered, "Good morning." He sat right up and wiped the sleep from his eyes. "I'm Rikki, and I was wondering if you could use a new pair of shoes?"

"Yeah, I could."

"What size are you, my friend?"

"Ten and a half," he said.

After I grabbed a few options from the back of my car, he said he liked the black and gray suede Nike Blazers. This was the first pair that went out from my personal collection, and it meant so much to me.

"Man, I love those on you. Do you mind if I take a picture?" I asked.

"Yeah, go ahead." He put out his foot.

As I snapped a picture, I thought about when I first bought the Blazers at a local shoe store. I even remembered what I would wear with them. By giving them away, those shoes had a new, deeper meaning to me now.

HAV A SOLE ON WHEELS

My buddy Dash has an athletic build with an intricate web of tattoos going up his arm to his neck. We had met at a Taco Tuesday party where we had first bonded over our love of fashion. Dash had a big heart, and with all the shoe donations coming in, he had been helping me organize the new storage bin.

The boxes of shoes inside the unit went clear up to the ceiling. In just two months, shoes had been donated from all over the country. While I was grateful for the support, I was also feeling overwhelmed.

"We need to get rid of shoes faster," I said.

"But how?"

"What if we host a pop-up event from the back of a truck?"

"That would be cool," Dash responded.

Having worked in commercial production for years, I had a relationship with Galpin Studio Rentals in Hollywood. When I told them what I wanted to do, they were more than willing to rent us a truck at a discounted rate. I picked a date and posted a caption on Instagram: "Join us this Saturday for our first Hav A Sole on Wheels!" I was shocked when more than fifty volunteers showed up for the event. Even my mom came out to help. As I stood on the tailgate of the truck, volunteers gathered around. I didn't have any experience in managing people or public speaking, but I was determined to give out shoes.

"First off, thank you for coming out today," I said. "To be honest, I have no idea what I'm doing." Everyone laughed. "But let's start by unloading the truck and sorting all the shoes by size and gender."

Later that day we gave out hundreds of shoes at a homeless shelter in Santa Monica. Not only was our first event a huge success but also we had put a big dent in our inventory.

NIKON

I was pouring a lot of my own money into Hav A Sole, and I knew I couldn't keep it up. A big break came when Cathi, the casting director who was always looking for opportunities for us, came across a casting call for any photographers who had an interesting story related to their craft. "This sounds like it might be a good fit for Hav A Sole," Cathi said.

I submitted an email telling the producer how I was using my photography to bring awareness to the homeless crisis. A few days later they, wanted to meet me. "We really love what you are doing," the producer said. "But can we hear more of your story?"

I took them all the way back to being nine years old, when the police woke me up on that horrible night Mom went to jail.

"Wow. What an amazing story you have, Rikki."

A few days later, I got a call back from the Nikon producer, saying they wanted to feature me in their new campaign, I Am Generation Image. He went on to explain that it would highlight a photographer's life through the lens of a camera. Not only would hundreds of thousands of people hear about Hav A Sole but also I would get paid for doing what I love while receiving a brand-new camera as well.

It was a dream come true. I had always wanted to get my photography noticed, and now Nikon was showing it for me, which was far better than getting a few likes on social media. Afterward the producer asked me where we could do an event.

"What about the shelter I lived in as a kid?"

"I love it," he exclaimed. "Could you get me a contact there?"

I gave him the name of an outreach coordinator at Clare Foundation, and the producer quickly secured a date and time.

On the day of the event, I pulled up in front of Clare Foundation in a truck. Mom, the volunteers, and I quickly set up as a camera crew filmed us. The residents at Clare formed a line alongside the sidewalk. When we started giving out shoes, the residents were extremely grateful, thanking us for bringing them shoes. I'll never forget one Hispanic woman who came up to Mom and me and said, "It really means a lot that you came here today." Tears filled her eyes. "I lost custody of my son because of my addiction, and he really hates me for it. But seeing you two doing this together gives me hope."

It occurred to me that us being there had more of an impact than any pair of shoes. No words were necessary. Our actions said it all.

TOYS FROM TONYA

Not long after the Nikon campaign, a teacher by the name of Tony reached out to me through social media and asked if I'd be willing to come speak to his classroom. I felt deeply honored. When I started Hav A Sole, I just wanted to give out my shoes, but now I was beginning to use my story as a tool to help others.

Standing in front of those eighth graders, my heart was racing. I knew it wasn't going to be easy to keep these young kids engaged, but as I told my truth, I could sense they were hanging on to my every word. My initial fear dissipated as I dropped into the present moment. This was my first time speaking, and I loved how it made me feel.

I was about to leave when a thirteen-year-old girl by the name of Tonya approached me. "Thank you for sharing your story," she said.

"Thank you for listening," I replied.

Tonya went on to tell me how she was once lived at the Union Rescue Mission on Skid Row before entering a foster home. I was familiar with the mission because we had done an event there in the past. "My dream is to go back and do something special for the kids one day," Tonya said.

"I love that idea." I paused. "What if we did a toy drive and Hav A Sole provides the shoes?"

"Really?" Her face lit up. "That would be awesome."

I reached out to my contact at the mission, and we scheduled an event for Christmas. For the next two months, Tonya and I collaborated over the phone, calling it Toys from Tonya. I posted about it on social media, and as a result, toys, clothing, and children's books started to come in. It was always surprising to me that people were so willing to help out.

On the day of the event, we all met at the mission downtown. The sun had just set, and shadows lurked in doorways while rows of tents lined the walls of vacant buildings. A woman shuffled by with a shopping cart, dragging one foot behind. When the security gate rolled up, I pulled my U-Haul into the subterranean garage. After setting up everything in the chapel, I told the director we had enough to provide each family with shoes, toys, and books.

As the families went through, I remember watching a young boy pick up a red car and hold it to his chest. His mom looked at me and said, "God bless you" before moving down the line.

I thought back to Christmas in transitional living when Mom got out of jail. I was ten years old, and volunteers had asked Mom what I wanted for Christmas.

"A basketball and shoes," I said. "That's all I want."

But on Christmas morning when I opened my gifts, there was a football and no shoes in sight. I remember the anger I felt at not getting what I wanted. I was determined to make sure the kids at the mission didn't feel the same disappointment that I had back then.

It was great night, and while we were cleaning up, a single mom with two teenage boys and two young girls arrived. The boys headed straight for the sneakers, but there was nothing left in their sizes. Before Elijah and his older brother, Malik, left, I asked them their sizes and promised to come back with shoes.

"Thank you for coming and Merry Christmas," the mom

said. I was blown away by their gratitude despite not getting any gifts.

As they walked out the door, I turned to Dash, who wore the same size as Elijah. "I bet you won't give him your shoes," I said, challenging him.

"If they fit, I will," he said, not hesitating.

I ran out the door and caught Elijah before he made it on the elevator. "Come on back. We might have a pair that fits you."

We got back into the chapel, where Dash began to untie his black-and-white Jordan Concords. If you know sneakers, this pair is one of the all-time greats. He slid the shoes over to Elijah.

"Do they fit?" I asked.

"Oh yeah. They fit, all right," Elijah said.

Bending over, Dash checked the toe. "Then they're all yours."

"Really? Thank you so much." Elijah was smiling from ear to ear. Tonya and the rest of the volunteers had tears in their eyes as Dash stood there in his socks.

"This is what the holidays are supposed to be about," someone said.

Five years later, Elijah sent us a direct message on Instagram and asked to volunteer at one of our events. On that day he helped us give out over one hundred pairs of shoes to homeless youth at the Covenant House. It served as a reminder that one small act of kindness can have a ripple effect, just like Becky's act of kindness had on me.

HURRICANE HARVEY

In 2017, over a span of two months, a series of disasters swept the globe. The evening news and social media bombarded us with images of hurricanes ripping through the Caribbean like freight trains, earthquakes in Mexico, and political unrest in the United States. By the time Hurricane Harvey flooded areas of Houston, we all had seen way too much suffering. The worst part for me was watching these tragedies and feeling like I couldn't do anything about them.

So when my friend Ayyde, a local radio host, texted me that a truck driver named Ben called in saying he was willing to drive his fifty-three-foot truck to Houston if someone could fill up the back with supplies, I replied immediately. "We have at least fifteen hundred pairs of sneakers we can give." Ayyde sent me

Ben's number and that same day we talked and launched a social media campaign to help get supplies to Houston.

The biggest challenge was finding a staging area in Los Angeles that could fit Ben's massive truck. We received several location leads, but none of them panned out. Discouraged, I was
about to push back the date, but at the last minute, Ed Barnett,
a board member, was able to get us access to a school parking
lot. With the location locked in, Hav A Sole flooded social media
with requests for volunteers and donations.

On the morning of September 23, we arrived at the parking
lot early, along with several other nonprofits, to set up tables
and booths. Ben arrived and jumped down from his truck. He
was a tall Hispanic guy with a neatly trimmed beard.

"What's up, Ben?" We hugged. "Thanks so much for doing
this."

"I felt like I had to do something."

I had plenty of experience giving shoes away, but nothing
had prepared me for the magnitude of support that came in that
day. Cars full of supplies started to arrive filled with everything
from water to diapers and food. A local nonprofit made over
five hundred kits filled with shampoo, soap, and other essen-

tials. We worked nonstop to pack, organize, and load boxes into Ben's truck, and in two days it was completely full.

***

Dash and I drove in the truck with Ben. It was a cloudless day, and the closer we got to Houston, the only vehicles we saw were tractor trailers and emergency vehicles. As we entered the city, everything seemed to turn a dull brownish gray. It was as if the world had lost all its color. The disaster had brought immense devastation. Uprooted trees and rows of washed-out vacant houses lined the streets. Drywall, tattered furniture, couches, and broken TVs littered the sidewalks. With abandoned cars on the side of the road, street signs knocked down, and traffic lights that didn't work, it looked apocalyptic.

A Houston nonprofit gave us access to a warehouse where we loaded our sneaker inventory into a smaller trailer. Our first stop was one of the city's libraries. When we got there, there was a line of mostly of Black and Brown people clear around the block. There were tables piled with clothes, blankets, books, and hygiene items under pop-up tents. On the other side of the parking lot were pickup trucks, SUVs, and a FEMA truck. We pulled all the way in the back and then leaped out and went straight to work.

With a distinct sense of urgency, we were unable to employ our unique style of fitting each person with a pair of shoes. We had to move fast. Two hours later, a steady stream of sweat was running down the back of my neck. The hot sun caused swarms of insects to circle around us. The line never seemed to get any shorter.

At one point, a heavyset Black woman came up to me. "Thank you for coming out here and doing this for us today."

We embraced before she left. My body relaxed from the amount of love that I felt coming from her. I imagined she was someone's mother, grandmother, sister, or friend. She gave me a dose of energy when I needed it the most. Sometimes it's that kind of moment that keeps you going. By the end of the day, Hav A Sole had given out over five hundred pairs of shoes.

Dash and I stayed with his cousin that night while Ben slept in his truck.

***

Early in the afternoon of the next day, we headed to Greenspoint Mall in a U-Haul truck. When we got there, it looked like there had to be at least three thousand people.

"Oh shit, look at that line," I said.

We parked all the way in the back and had started organizing the shoes when a lanky, Hispanic teenager approached us. "Do you guys need any help?" he asked.

"No, were good," Dash said.

He turned to walk away. "Wait, wait. Hold on," I said. "What's your name?"

"Javier."

"Hey, Javier. What are you doing here?"

"My grandma's house was destroyed in the storm, and my parents are in the back of the line trying to get supplies."

"Oh man, I'm so sorry."

"I just want to do something to help my people and the city."

"Do you speak Spanish, Javier?"

"Yup. I do."

"It would be great if you can help us translate," I said.

"No problem."

Javier worked with us, giving out shoes and translating when needed for five hours straight. The sun beat down on our backs.

It was grueling work. Sometimes I'd be overwhelmed by the suffering of people who were already struggling when the hurricane hit. Before Javier left, he introduced us to his mom and the rest of his family. I made sure to give them all new shoes. It was the least I could do. After finishing for the day, Dash and I headed for Dallas while Ben made his way back to Los Angeles. It hardly seemed like what we did was enough, but it was good knowing that Hav A Sole had stepped up in some small way.

The next morning, on October 2, we woke up to the devastating news of a mass shooting in Las Vegas. Someone had opened fire with assault rifles on a live concert, killing sixty-one and injuring over eight hundred concertgoers. All the insanity going on in the world broke my heart. Sadly, all I could do was wonder what was going to happen next.

SWEAT EQUITY

I had no idea how much work went into launching a start-up.
The money I had made from Nikon was gone, and all my pay-
checks from doing background work in commercials was going
into Hav A Sole. But I felt as if I had finally found my purpose,
and giving out shoes was all I wanted to do. A break came when
I received an email from NationSwell, a production company that profiled impact-driven stories. When we talked on the
phone, the producer said they wanted to do a small five-minute
piece profiling Hav A Sole. Although it wasn't a paying gig, it
was perfect timing. A high-quality video could not only bring
awareness to our mission but also help us to raise money. Plans
were made for a director by the name of Sean Ryon to came out
from New York and film what we were doing.

A few days later, Dash and I were sorting through boxes in our eight-by-ten storage unit. It was hardly enough space to hold all the incoming donations. Compressed cardboard boxes were stacked on top of each other from floor to ceiling. In order to get ready for an event, we had to drag each box out into the hallway and pull the different sizes. It was hard work. I would be in the unit for hours, with sweat dripping down my back. The storage unit doubled as our office. It was where we'd problem solve, brainstorm, and figure out next steps. When it was time to take a break, I grabbed a bottle of water. "I don't know how we're going to keep this up," I said.

"What do you mean?" Dash asked.

"I mean financially. I only have one hundred sixty-three dollars left in the bank account. We really need to find ways to raise money."

We started to run through a list of potential donors when I thought about Steve, a successful, down-to-earth businessman in the Bay Area whom we had met two years before. The following week I emailed him and set up a meeting.

Meanwhile, Sean from NationSwell arrived, and I instantly loved his enthusiasm. He was young, creative, and eager to do his job. "I want to film you guys doing one of your events."

"How about a Hav A Sole on Wheels?" I said. "We could do it downtown."

On the day of the event, I pulled up in a rental truck, and over thirty volunteers had showed up to help. Wearing my favorite black T-shirt with LOVE written across the front and a straw hat to protect me from the sun, I jumped out of the truck. We set up the pop-up tent and chairs in the empty parking lot. My background as a production assistant had prepared me for work like this.

Meanwhile, a few volunteers went out to inform people on the street that we were giving away shoes. In less than fifteen minutes, over a hundred people stood on the sidewalk. It reminded me of the times when I stood in line for a limited pair of Jordans, hoping that I would not be one of the many people who would walk away empty-handed. But on the day of our event, I was hoping to get all the people in line a new pair of shoes.

For the next two hours, Sean rushed around with a camera perched on his shoulder, filming the entire event. One woman with long gray hair pulled up in a wheelchair with swollen feet. I'll never forget the volunteer who worked with her.

"It's too narrow for my foot," she said, giving the shoe back.

"Let's try another pair," he said. Over and over, he patiently stayed with her until he found a shoe that fit her foot.

By the end of the day, we had given out over two hundred pairs. Sean came up to me and said, "I've got some amazing footage here."

"That's great, man," I said, giving him a hug.

The next day Sean went back to New York, but he kept me updated on his progress. A few weeks went by, and the meeting with Steve was getting closer. I was hoping to get the video beforehand so that I could show it to him while I was there.

This was a huge opportunity, and I didn't want to go alone, so I asked Mom if she wanted to go with me. "Of course," she said. "We can drive up the day before and stay with my friends."

On the way up to the Bay Area, we used the six-hour drive to rehearse. Mom used her writing skills to help me create a script. I had butterflies, but I knew that in many ways, Hav A Sole was pushing me past my fears and allowing me to do things outside of my comfort zone.

"Let's go through your presentation again," Mom said.

"Let me walk you through our program budget for 2017. We

have big plans."

After every run-through, Mom would give me feedback so that I could tighten up my speech. We practiced over and over, until I knew exactly what I was going to say.

"Do you think we'll have the video from Sean in time?" Mom asked.

"I hope so," I said, knowing that the NationSwell piece could help.

As planned, we spent the night at Mom's friend's house. The following morning, I woke up to an email from Sean that had come in while I was asleep. I was so touched that Sean had stayed up the entire night working on a rough cut so that we'd have something to present to Steve. It was called *The Sneaker Saint.*

I joined Mom in the kitchen. "Look what Sean emailed me last night."

After I played the video, she had tears in her eyes. "That's so good," she said. "Steve is going to love it."

Just before 9:00 a.m., when we arrived in downtown San Francisco, a metered parking space opened up right in front of the building. "I'll take that as a good sign," I said, looking at

Mom.

Staying true to the Hav A Sole brand, I wore a pair of my favorite Nike Dunks, jeans, and a button-up, long-sleeve shirt. A few minutes later we were riding the elevator up to the eleventh floor. My clammy hands carried a manila folder that held our budget and a list of our board of directors. My mind quickly went over the script. The perfectionist in me didn't want to forget any of my lines, so I kept repeating them inside my head.

When we checked in with Steve's secretary, I told her I had a video presentation and asked her for the Wi-Fi password.

"We have a television that might work better," she said, leading us down the hall.

The conference room had breathtaking views of the Bay Bridge. As the minutes passed, my stomach did major flips. Sensing my nervousness, Mom said, "You're going to be great."

A few minutes later, Steve came in dressed in casual business attire.

"Rikki, my man. How's everything going?" he asked, giving me a hug.

"Things are great, Steve," I said. "I'm so excited to tell you what we've been up to with Hav A Sole."

"Love to hear it." He sat across from us.

After briefly catching up on all our events, I said, "I got something to show you, Steve." I pressed play and the video began. It was almost six minutes long. As I watched him in my peripheral vision, I sensed that Steve was enjoying the film.

When it was over, he said, "Man, that was powerful."

"I was honored that they asked me to be profiled, but I want to tell you about our plans for growing the organization even more." I took a deep breath and repeated my well-rehearsed lines. "Although we're getting plenty of shoes in from Nike, Puma, and other partners, we want to impact more people." I might have appeared calm on the outside, but inside my heart was racing.

"How can I help?" he asked.

"I need you to cover half of our 2017 budget." I slid the document across the table.

Steve looked at it for a few seconds and then without any hesitation said, "Okay, I'll do it."

I had rehearsed my lines so many times that his answer didn't register, and I kept talking until Mom said, "Rikki, he said he would do it." I looked at Mom, then back at Steve. I was at a loss for words. I had just asked for a lot of money, and he had agreed.

"It's good work you're doing out there, and I want to be a part of it," he said.

"Wow! Thank you so much, Steve." I circled the conference table and gave him a big hug. "Your support means everything to me."

"I'll send you a check. Just keep up the good work."

Later, on the drive home, I was ecstatic. At one point Mom turned down the volume on the radio and asked, "Can you believe what just happened?"

"We are so blessed."

If it wasn't for Steve's generous donation, Hav A Sole might have folded. Eight years later, he still continues to support the mission.

HEADQUARTERS

I was still living in the guesthouse in Culver City. While the location was great, the four-hundred-square-foot space was starting to feel claustrophobic. I couldn't get organized. There was paperwork on the floor. I had to use my computer while propped up on my bed. And while I had a storage unit, shoes often ended up coming home with me. It was clear that if I wanted Hav A Sole to grow, I needed a bigger place where I could both work and live. As the founder, I had to know when to take action, and this was one of those times.

I shared my idea with Mom, and one day not long after, she called with a lead. "You should check out this place downtown," she said.

I made an appointment for us to see it that same day. Driving downtown, there were scattered tents, plywood, and home-made shelters lining the walls of industrial buildings, with concrete walls covered in graffiti. I could feel the deprivation in those handmade shelters like a sucking wind. It triggered my old feelings of scarcity, and I wanted to do more for people who were living on the streets, but I reminded myself that Hav A Sole was at the very least bringing awareness to the homeless crisis, and that would have to be enough for now.

We pulled up in front of a gated compound, and inside were two large brick buildings. Mom raised an eyebrow. "It's smack dab in the center of all the homeless encampments," she said.

"Isn't that where Hav A Sole needs to be?"

"I guess." But she didn't sound convincing.

We met Angie, the women I spoke to on the phone. "I have two vacancies I can show you today," she said, leading us down a long corridor.

I liked both lofts, but the downstairs unit had a parking space right in front of the entrance, which meant I could bring shoes directly from my car. It had cement floors with exposed brick walls, built-in shelves, and wooden beams.

I moved in the following month. That first night in Hav

A Sole's new headquarters was strange. I wasn't used to having fourteen-foot-high ceilings or room to move around, but I quickly got used it. In fact, we expanded so rapidly that I would be forced to move again. The unit I moved into was in the same compound and had multiple levels with exposed pipes, concrete floors, and a southwestern flair. I dedicated the downstairs area to separating shoes and storing them in bins on industrial shelves that lined the wall. It had multiple closets where I could store incoming boxes of donated shoes. It also had a nook for an office where I set up a desk and a file cabinet. Upstairs, light streamed in from the large windows, and there was an enclosed sleeping area that could remain out of sight. It was a perfect space to invite sponsors and donors and to hold board meetings. Hav A Sole never felt so legitimate.

KARA

I first met Kara in 2018 when she volunteered at a Hav A Sole event. She was in her early thirties, originally from the Philippines, and moved here when she was seven. She had long silky black hair, an infectious smile, and a great sense of humor.

After several months of hanging out, Kara and I were at my place sharing a pizza when she asked the dreaded question: "So what are we doing here? I mean, where do you think this relationship is going?" She looked at me with dark, searching eyes.

I took a sip of water to stall for time. It had been a nice evening, and I didn't want to ruin it with any talk of commitment. On the other hand, I wanted to be honest with her. "I just don't see myself being anyone's boyfriend right now."

"I want to be with you all the time."

"See, that *really doesn't* sound good to me." Spending my days and nights with someone for the rest of my life was the last thing I wanted to do.

"Oh. Okay." I could hear the disappointment in her voice.

"Do we have to figure this out right now?" I asked.

She stared at the TV. "I guess not."

Meanwhile, I had been volunteering with Good City Mentors, an organization that mentored youth in local high schools. The week after the awkward conversation with Kara, the founder, Brian Larrabee, informed all the volunteers that he was hosting a special meeting at the Netflix building across the street from Bernstein High.

The offices had high ceilings, hardwood floors, and sweeping glass windows with views of the city. Three steps dropped down into a sunken conference room with two rows of opposite-facing curved oatmeal-colored cushions. The seating configuration made it feel extremely intimate for the twenty mentors there that day. Brian greeted everyone in his usual enthusiastic fashion.

"First, I want to thank all of you for showing up every week," Brian said. "When I started Good City Mentors, the only plan I had was to enlist volunteers like yourselves. Some of the kids we work with have grim living situations with parents who are addicts or incarcerated, and some of the kids are even homeless." Brian leaned forward. "But today, instead of talking about the kids, I'd like to talk about where you think *you* might be holding back and what it would take for you to change."

I shifted uneasily in my seat. I knew I was holding back when it came to Kara. It felt like the Netflix spotlight was beaming down on my head, with me in the leading role of some rom-com where the man refuses to commit to the cute girl. "I've been dating someone for six months, and I'm afraid to commit to her," I confessed to the entire room.

All eyes were on me. When some of the people nodded, I felt safe. I didn't feel judged.

"What do you think it would take for you to change that?" Brian asked.

I paused for a moment. "I guess facing my fears and not running from a good thing."

Brian smiled. "Sometimes just saying the truth out loud helps you to see things clearer."

The meeting felt like a group therapy session that got me

thinking about some of my issues. *Why did I keep swatting away commitment like an annoying gnat? What was stopping me? What was I afraid of? That Kara would ask too much of me?*

Later that night, Kara and I were watching TV at my place. During the commercial she got up to go the bathroom and had almost reached the door when I asked, "Will you be my girlfriend?"

She turned and her face lit up with a big smile. "What did you say?"

"You heard me."

"I'll be right back." When she returned, she sat beside me and looked me right in the eye. "Did you mean what you just said?" she asked.

"Yeah, I meant it."

"Yes, I will be your girl." She kissed me. "I love you so much."

"I love you too."

***

I thought committing to a relationship would make things easier, so I couldn't understand why Kara was angry all the time. A month later I was on the couch, and she stood in front of me with her arms crossed. "You never go out with me," she said, her lips pulled tight.

"What are you talking about?"

"You only have time for Hav A Sole," she said. "You're supposed to be my boyfriend, but we're never seen out together."

"Kara, you know that I don't drink or party." I was irritated now. This was why I didn't let people in. They always ended up having high expectations of me.

Her brow creased. "I think it's time for me to figure out what I want to do here," she said.

"Okay. That's fine. I'm not going to stand in your way." If she wanted to move on, I wasn't going to stop her.

"Will you go to couples counseling with me?" she asked.

There was a long silence. The invitation hung there in the room as I thought about my options. It was so much easier doing it alone, but I was at a point in my life when I wanted to stop running. I was thirty-six. I didn't want to wake up one day bitter, alone, and filled with regret. Kara held the kind of promise of a future that I could no longer resist.

But was I willing to do the work?

I had been to therapy only a few times, when I was a kid. Mom made me go when I started getting in trouble at school. She thought if I had someone to talk to, it might help with my anger issues. Back then, I had no idea that talking to someone could be useful. Now here I was, decades later, willing to do the work. "Sure," I said. "Let's do it."

We met our therapist via Zoom. He was an older white guy with glasses. "Why don't we go through some of your history," he said. "Kara, you go first."

As Kara talked about her insecurities growing up, I could relate. There had been a lot of secrecy in her family, and although the circumstances were different, the outcome was the same. Fear of rejection. Fear of being hurt. Fear of taking risks.

When it was my turn, I told the therapist about the nine-year-old boy who woke up surrounded by police when Mom went to jail. As I recalled the painful memories, the skin on the back of my neck tightened. There was so much to tell that I began pacing myself, breathing in and out. Although I had shared my story before with the youth in the mentorship program, there was much more at stake this time. This was someone I thought I wanted to spend my life with.

When I was done, the therapist said, "Wow, Rikki, you've been through a lot. It's not surprising that you both are struggling to trust one another."

"What do you mean?" Kara asked.

"Well, I think you had so much instability as children, your trust was broken. And maybe when you are getting mad at Rikki, his response is to shut down."

Kara started to sob. "I'm so sorry. I didn't realize my past affected me this way."

"It's okay, honey." I stroked her shoulder.

"And for you, Rikki, I think you're using avoidance as a survival mechanism."

I nodded. "That makes total sense."

"What are we supposed to do?" Kara asked.

"Don't you think it's about time you both allow yourselves to have a good thing?" the therapist said.

I looked over at Kara. "We owe it to ourselves to be happy," I said.

For years I thought my past didn't need to be explored, but therapy not only offered me some clarity but also showed me that it's never too late to start working on yourself.

BOOK RELEASE

Mom was now in her sixties. She had lines around her eyes, and her hair had all but turned gray. She was still working in mental health and was writing her first memoir. We were having breakfast one morning when I asked, "How's your book coming along?"

"Doing revisions, but it's almost there," she said. Her face lit up anytime she talked about her writing. She'd had me review some of the chapters, and I almost couldn't believe she was putting her deepest, darkest secrets out there for anyone to read.

"What do you think Dad's going to say when he reads it?" I asked.

"I just hope he doesn't sue me."

"You think he would?"

"Who knows?" She shrugged. "But just in case, I changed his name."

I could still remember a time when Dad was my absolute hero. I have memories of him with his curly black Afro and his thick arms and chest and how everyone laughed at his jokes. He always loved watching sports on the weekends and taught me things about basketball whenever a Lakers game came on. "See how Magic and Kareem dominate the floor?" he'd say, pointing to the screen. "No one can stop them. No one." I took in all his observations as law.

However, despite those fond memories, I could never reconcile how my hero could just disappear from my life save for Thanksgiving dinners.

One day, Mom called to say that she had a publisher for the book.

"You did it," I said.

"I know. I know. It's crazy."

"I'm so proud of you."

"Thank you, Rikki. I'm blown away. But I need you to shoot the cover for me." Her vision for the cover was a revolver sitting on top of a load of laundry. "Since I'm about to air my dirty laundry to the world, I think it's the perfect image," she explained.

When the book came out on Mother's Day in 2020, everyone was excited to read it. I read it, my brother read it, my nephews and nieces read it. Everyone was supportive of Mom following her dream.

A few months later, while I was doing inventory at Hav A Sole headquarters, I got an unexpected call from Dad. "I just finished your mom's book," he said.

I sat down to brace myself in case he was about to vent. "Oh? So how did you like it?"

"It was brutally honest, but I actually liked it a lot." Dad let out a sigh. "It made me think about a few things that happened when you were a kid that I had completely forgotten about."

My mind wandered back to when we got evicted and were living in the car, with Dad leaving me alone while he was drinking at Joe's bar. I thought about being on welfare and not being able to afford shoes as well as all the times Dad didn't come to visit when he said he would.

"I'm really sorry for not being a better father to you, son."

I was stunned. I felt a pinch in my throat. It wasn't in Dad's nature to apologize or even to acknowledge his past behavior, but he seemed to be getting softer in his old age.

I had spent most of my life compartmentalizing everything, but with those few words from my father, I sensed a deep well of old pain at my center, like an umbilical cord linking me to all my early childhood trauma. It was a dark place that I hadn't entirely unearthed because I was afraid if I did, I would lose my shit. As a result, I had been plagued by a constant sadness that followed me like my own personal rain cloud. I felt it every time I slowed down or hit a wall, and I would quickly divert my attention elsewhere. It may have been the reason for my sneaker obsession or why I wouldn't commit to any one girl for so long, but part of what was driving my life was the pain of my childhood. While my mother had made amends after getting out of jail, my father, not so much.

"I love you, son," he said.

I felt an opening in my chest, a cracking of the wall. Not because I was flooded with an absolute healing but because hearing him take responsibility for his part in my childhood trauma helped me drop a mighty big rock that I had been carrying for a long time.

In that moment it became crystal clear. I had always loved Dad, and I always would.

MAMBA MENTALITY

Once or twice a year, Hav A Sole sets out on a cross-country road trip delivering shoes to youth in designated cities. We track everything, whether it's picking up shoe donations or going to a shelter and sharing the stories on social media.

Dash and I were excited about our eighth road trip, which would take us all the way to Chicago during the NBA All-Star weekend.

On January 26, I woke up to TMZ's website reporting that Lakers basketball legend Kobe Bryant, along with eight others, had died in a helicopter crash. My heart dropped. It couldn't be true. I turned to Kara, who was sound asleep next to me. "Honey, wake up! They say Kobe died in a helicopter crash."

She bolted straight up in bed. "What? No way."

I turned on the news, but there was nothing about the crash. I was hopeful that TMZ was wrong. Kara joined me on the couch, and when the local news cut away to a live crash scene on the side of a mountain, my ears started ringing. Kara kept saying, "No, no, no."

But it was true. Kobe Bryant; his thirteen-year-old daughter, Gianna; and seven others were traveling to a basketball tournament when the pilot crashed in thick fog. There were no survivors. My chest felt as if it was gripped by a vise. I started to cry as tears fell from Kara's eyes. We held each other in a tight embrace. Kobe was gone. How could that be? He was Superman, and superheroes aren't supposed to die.

On the court, Kobe was known to be fearless and cold-blooded, much like the Black Mamba moniker he was associated with. Off the court, Kobe was relentless when it came to helping homeless youth. He even formed the Kobe and Vanessa Bryant Foundation, which was dedicated to improving the lives of families in need. Over the past year, I had been trying to secure a meeting with Kobe to discuss getting his support for Hav A Sole. I was certain that if we had a global icon like Kobe endorsing us, it would help us do greater things.

The Staples Center in downtown Los Angeles (renamed in 2021 as the Crypto.com Arena) was home to the Los Angeles Lakers and was where Kobe had spent his entire twenty-year career. The center was only a mile away from Hav A Sole's head-quarters, so Mom, Kara, Dash, and I drove there the following day to pay our respects. Seeing how fans had laid photographs, flowers, and banners in front of the stadium made his death even seem more real. Seeing one of Kobe's jerseys under a wreath, I was struck with an idea. I turned to Dash. "We need to dedicate this road trip to Kobe. He wore number eight, and this is our eighth road trip."

Dash loved the idea. In fact, we even extended our trip to include Lower Merion, Kobe's old high school in Philadelphia. By dedicating road trip number eight to Kobe, it held a deeper meaning for us now.

We hit the road on February 1 in a rental van packed with sneakers. Our first three stops were Dallas, Memphis, and In-dianapolis for which we partnered with NBA teams to give out shoes.

***

February 16, 2020

All-Star Game

Walking up to the United Center, the home of the Chicago Bulls, I felt like a kid. I was wearing a Kobe shirt, and Dash had on his Kobe jersey. We were there to represent. In the lobby was a Michael Jordan statue that was built in 1994. It was designed to create the illusion of flight, with Jordan sailing through the air with a basketball in his hand. The statue sat on a block of granite inscribed with the words: "The best there ever was. The best there ever will be."

All of a sudden, Steve Simon walked up dressed in a white button-up shirt, a blazer, and jeans. "Hey, guys. You made it," he said, giving us both a hug.

"Hey, Steve. How's it going?"

"I want to show you around."

He escorted us through an unmarked door into a maze of corridors that eventually led onto the court. There were a few players scattered on the baseline. I noticed Damian Lillard of the Portland Trailblazers with his closely cropped beard and tattoos running up both arms. I went to school with someone he knew, so I felt comfortable going up to him. "Hey, Dame, we have a mutual friend," I said.

"Oh yeah? Who's that?" He turned to me.

I told him about my friend who had helped him produce some of his music.

"Oh yeah. He's a good dude."

"Do you mind if I get an autograph?" I said.

"No problem." He signed his name on my Kobe shirt.

My eyes grew wide when Russell Westbrook and James Harden of the Houston Rockets came over. A few moments later, LeBron strutted over and joined in the conversation. There I was standing on the court with some of the greatest players in the NBA. I couldn't believe it.

As a kid, all I wanted to do was play basketball, not just because I loved the sport but because I admired the athletes who pursued their dreams. Somehow Hav A Sole had given me the opportunity to stand among some of the biggest NBA legends in the game. I was wrapped up in the moment until security told us we had to go.

As Dash and I walked away, I said, "Oh my God. That really just happened?"

"That was so crazy." We both laughed.

***

Two days after the All-Star Game, we arrived at Lower Merion High School. We still had no real plan in place, but we were determined to go. As Dash and I approached the front of the school, we saw a tall staff member with his brow creased and his arms crossed over his chest standing out front. We walked right up to him and introduced ourselves. "To make a long story short, we drove here all the way from LA," I said.

He cut me off. "Say no more and follow me." He took us inside to the Kobe Bryant gymnasium. It was the same place where Kobe had scored 2,883 points during his high school career. I felt deeply honored to be standing in the same gym where he had played.

"Are you guys coming to the game tonight?" the staff member asked.

"What game?"

"Our varsity team is in the playoffs, and its only five dollars to get in."

Dash and I looked at each other and smiled. "Yeah, we'll be

here for sure."

Later that night as I watched the team play—the sound of shouting, a referee's whistle piecing the air, the ball being dribbled down the court, and sneakers squeaking across the hardwood floors—it was music to my ears. I love basketball. Whether it's a high school varsity team, an All-Star Game, or just playing in the park. I love it, because in many ways it's what saved me from myself. I often released my anger, sadness, and disappointment on the court. Road trip number eight was worth every dollar spent, every mile traveled, and every storm we passed through. There was no better place to process Kobe's loss than by watching Lower Merion win a playoff game.

Rest in peace, Kobe. Mamba out.

THE PANDEMIC

As the coronavirus raged across the globe and we were all ordered to shelter in place, Los Angeles became a ghost town. The freeways were deserted, schools and businesses closed down, and the sidewalks were empty. We had to cancel shoe giveaways, and the biggest blow of all was having to cancel our annual fundraiser. With all the uncertainty, I wanted to do something. But what could I do from inside Hav A Sole headquarters? That's when I thought of Ivan, an LAPD officer I knew from collaborating on events. I got him on the phone.

"I want to do something for all the kids who are stuck inside," I said.

Ivan was the founder of the Watts Skills Academy, a basketball program that provided mentorship to kids in Watts. Initially, Ivan started the program with a desire to create better community relations with the police, but for Ivan, it was more than that. After doing an event with his kids, we stayed in touch, either by phone or sometimes we'd play basketball together.

"What do you have in mind, Rikki?" he asked.

"How about we challenge your kids to a weeklong exercise program, with a different workout each day? They can post on social media and tag Hav A Sole so that we can track their progress. When they finish, we'll drop off a fresh pair of sneakers right to their doorstep."

"Man, I love that idea. Let's do it."

"Can you reach out to the parents and get their sizes?"

"No problem, but most of our kids live in dangerous neighborhoods, so we'd have to go with you to deliver the shoes."

Ivan put the word out to all the parents, and the kids were excited to have something to do. I loved seeing them post their crunches, push-ups, and jumping jacks on Instagram.

***

George Floyd's death occurred during that time. The gut-wrenching nine-minute and twenty-nine-second video of a white police officer kneeling on the neck of a Black man was captured by a seventeen-year-old bystander on her phone. I was outraged to see this happen again.

It brought back recent memories of when Dash and I were in Charlotte, North Carolina. We were in a parking lot sorting shoes from the back of our van when multiple police cars surrounded us. I was sitting in the driver's seat when a cop walked up and put a gun to my head. Another cop pulled Dash from the passenger seat and placed him in handcuffs.

"What are y'all doing here?" the cop yelled in my face.

"We're delivering shoes to a local shelter." My heart was racing, but I remained calm. I explained that I was the founder of a nonprofit that gave out shoes. I had given the Hav A Sole pitch so many times before but never to a cop who held a gun to my head.

I could almost feel the collective exhale as they began to realize we weren't criminals after all. Their reason for rolling up on us like that? Someone had called in a robbery in progress. I understand they had a job to do; however, the way they handcuffed Dash seemed racially motivated to me.

Around the time of the George Floyd protests, I was being

escorted by two police cars into the projects of South Central. The area was filled with small single-house dwellings, and there was no one on the streets. A basketball court sat empty.

We pulled up to a small two-toned house with towels on a slack laundry line. Black wrought iron screens covered the doors and windows. This was where Meryland, a fourteen-year-old boxer, lived with her family. This was a girl who had dreams of competing in the Junior Olympics and who had already won two silver gloves.

Meryland and her entire family came outside to greet Ivan and me. We were masked and maintained a respectful distance while they stood inside their yard.

"I brought you some Jordans," I said, passing the box over the fence.

She flipped open the lid. "These are awesome. I love them," she said.

All day long we delivered shoes, and by the time we gave out our last pair, the sun had already gone down.

I turned to Ivan and said, "What an incredible day that was."

"Thank you for showing our kids some love. They really need it right now."

We hugged and said our goodbyes. On my drive home, I couldn't help but think about how different my life had become. I used to run from the police, but on this particular day, I had worked alongside them to help a few kids.

NEVER TOO LATE

Six years into creating Hav A Sole, Brian asked me to share my life story at Bernstein High. I stood in front of the kids and said, "I know what it's like to come from a broken home. I know what it's like to be homeless. I know what it's like to not want to go to school, but I've learned that all those seemingly bad things that happened in my past have shaped my journey in helping others today."

Following my talk, a kid named DJ asked to speak with me privately. We went outside to the quad. "I'm thinking of joining a gang," he said. "I want to get my money up."

I knew he was talking about selling drugs, and two things struck me: the directness of his words, and the courage it had taken for him to approach me. DJ explained that he lived with his single mother, who couldn't afford to buy him the nice things he wanted. I knew exactly what that felt like, and I wanted to help. I said, "Before you join a gang, why don't you come work for me at Hav A Sole for a couple of hours? I'll pay you fifty dollars an hour."

"For real?"

"Yes. For real."

DJ showed up the following week after school and helped with sneaker inventory. I don't know if it kept him from joining a gang, but as a result, other kids heard about it and asked if they could work for Hav A Sole as well.

A week later, Dash and I were at headquarters when it struck me how we could help more kids. "What if we created a paid internship for the youth at Bernstein High? We could show them how we run Hav A Sole and bring in guest speakers to do workshops."

Dash nodded his head thoughtfully. "I like that idea."

Things moved quickly from there. We reached out to our board members, who also wanted to help. Ed said he'd host a financial literacy workshop. Brennan offered to discuss LinkedIn as a networking tool. Nohan offered to do a résumé-building workshop, and Mom said she'd speak about resilience.

We set up the Hav A Sole headquarters like a classroom, with a whiteboard, computers, and notebooks for each kid. Five recently graduated eighteen-year-olds from Bernstein High would comprise the inaugural group. On their first day, we went over their roles and responsibilities. They would come in three days a week for a comprehensive educational program.

One of the first speakers was Mom. She stood up front dressed in a jean jacket and black leggings. The kids were fanned out across the room. For nearly three decades, she had been sharing her story in juvenile hall, prisons, and AA meetings. I'd heard it many times before, but this time it felt a little more special.

The first time I heard her tell her story, it gave me so much more insight into her life. Why she did drugs. Why she desperately clung to a marriage that was broken. Up until that point, I didn't know that trauma was intergenerational. Then when Mom got sober and began to show up in her life, it changed the trajectory of our family's lineage.

Standing in front of the kids, Mom took a gulp from her water bottle and said, "I had a lot of trauma in my childhood. My mother was a schizophrenic. My father was an alcoholic.

We didn't talk about any of it because of the stigma attached to mental illness. When I was seven years old, my mother killed herself."

The room was silent.

"I swore I'd never be like my mom," she continued, "but sometimes when you say *never*, it's like giving the universe the exact coordinates to where you will later land." She paused to let that sink in. "At thirty-eight, I had a drug-induced psychotic break and ended up shooting my husband's mistress in the arm."

The kids' eyes widened.

She went on to tell her entire story. How she went to jail and to transitional living, what it was like being a single mom on welfare, and how hard it was being poor. "It has taken a lot of time to heal the damage that was caused by my addiction," she said, "but recovery changes things. I don't have all the answers. Nobody does. Not your parents. Not your teachers. Not even the social workers. But I do know one thing. Keeping everything pent-up inside damn near killed me. So if you're suffering and feel alone, don't be afraid to ask for help."

When she was done, the energy in the room had shifted. It

was heavy with the truth.

***

A few days later when I talked to the kids, I was honest with them as well. I told them I hadn't graduated high school. I wasn't trying to negate the importance of an education, but I wanted to show them that despite having had a shitload of adversity, I had managed to create Hav A Sole. I knew they lived against the backdrop of poverty, tense race relations, and limited resources. I knew they might never see or hear a role model with a background similar to theirs, so I wanted to give them hope.

One of them was a soft-spoken Hispanic kid named Jeckson. I could tell he was serious in the way he asked questions, listened, and took notes.

Steve spoke to the kids via Zoom. He talked about the importance of family, which prompted Jeckson to reveal that he had a brother in prison. The whole room grew quiet. "I'm worried I'm going to end up just like him," he said.

"My brother went to prison years ago," I said. "But he's doing okay now."

Jeckson's eyes narrowed, and he studied my face.

Steve asked Jeckson, "What did he go in for?"

"Drug-related charges."

Everyone nodded because we all knew someone who had struggled with drugs. Steve gave Jeckson his number and told him to call so that they could talk. I would later discover that Steve also wrote to Jeckson's brother in prison. I was moved by Steve's thoughtfulness and generosity.

The following week, Ed facilitated a workshop on financial literacy. Ed was a money manager for professional athletes. The kids were riveted and so was I. Ed was someone I respected deeply, and he insisted that education was the key to success. The kids were all nodding their heads in agreement. I shifted uneasily in my chair. I wondered why I had always framed not finishing school in a positive light. Yes, I had started a nonprofit, but wasn't being a role model also being someone who never gives up?

Shortly thereafter, Steve asked me if I had ever thought about going back to school and getting my GED.

"Yeah, it's been on my mind lately," I replied.

"Maybe you should look into it."

I knew that one of our partners, the Covenant House, offered unhoused youth the opportunity to get their diplomas. I was good friends with Anthony, the Covenant House's outreach coordinator. I called him and asked, "Do you know how I'd go about getting my GED?"

"Let me check around and get back to you," he said.

He spoke with the Covenant House's CEO, Bill. A couple of weeks later, Bill not only offered me access to their education program but also insisted on it.

"Call Miss B., and she'll walk you through the next steps," Anthony said.

Miss B. was Hispanic, with bright-green hair. When we met, I told her that in my senior year of high school, I had to transfer to Hamilton High and ended up dropping out.

"Let's start by getting your high school transcripts and having you test so that we can see where you are in math and English," she said with a reassuring smile.

I scored pretty well on my tests, and when the transcripts came, I was shocked to discover that I had been very close to graduating.

"I'm going to have you work on assignments, and you can go at your own pace," Miss B. said.

"What if I need help?" The same insecurity I carried in high school was back.

"Call me anytime," she said.

In the past, I had never thought my teachers cared about my progress, but Miss B. regularly checked in to see how I was coming along. Her genuine concern motivated me to get up early each morning to do my homework. I studied new topics, including restorative justice, along with the basics such as world history.

Every day I worked through the tedious lessons. Every time I completed an assignment, I felt one step closer to my goal. Exactly twenty years after dropping out, during the height of the COVID-19 pandemic, I graduated from high school, proving to myself and to all the kids I would mentor that it is never too late to accomplish your goals.

DREAM OUT LOUD

Like many other businesses during the pandemic, Hav A Sole was struggling financially. A lot of funding had dried up or had been redirected toward basic needs such as housing or food for the homeless. Then one day I received an email from Michelle, a producer on *The Ellen DeGeneres Show*, asking me if I could talk. The show was well known for interviewing celebrities, but it also highlighted people who were making a difference within their communities. Michelle told me over Zoom that they'd like to have me on as a guest. My heart nearly leaped out of my chest.

The crazy thing was that just the year before, Mom and I had gotten tickets to a taping of the show with hopes of somehow getting Hav A Sole on Ellen's radar. I had brought some Hav A

Sole merchandise that I was going to try to get to Ellen, though I had no idea how I was going to accomplish that. As I sat in the audience, absorbed in the frenetic energy and music of a live taping, I imagined myself sitting across from Ellen. *What would that be like? How would I feel?*

Afterward, I was able to give the show's emcee, Twitch, one of my Hav A Sole hats and told him about the company. Twitch was really kind, and since he was a fan of a good pair of sneakers, he started following us on social media. The following day, Mom submitted a pitch for the third time to be a guest on the show.

Now, two weeks after talking to Michelle, Mom and I were headed to the studio where Michelle escorted us to the green room. She explained they would be filming two episodes back-to-back, and Mom would be in the audience during both shows.

An hour later I was backstage listening to Ellen's voice boom over the speakers as she talked to her audience about Hav A Sole. My chest rose, and I took a big breath. It felt sacred to stand on the other side of a vision I had had just the year before. It felt like a magician had said, "Abracadabra" and had conjured up this moment. *Is this really happening? Was I really on* The

Ellen DeGeneres Show?

I was, because the next thing I knew, Ellen said, "Now please join me in welcoming Rikki Mendias." Blinking back the bright lights, I had a brief feeling of transcendence as I stepped out. Everything slowed down. It felt as if I was weightless and that I had entered another world. The set was decorated in bright oranges and browns for autumn. Some of the audience was live, and some were on television monitors watching from home because of COVID-19. Ellen greeted me with a socially distanced elbow bump, and I sat down right across from her. It was surreal. There was a humming inside my chest.

I told Ellen my personal story, just as I had told it so many times before. I felt no shame, no embarrassment, and no regret. It was something I had come not only to accept but also to understand that it had me into the man I was today.

Ellen then said, "And I understand your mom is here?" The camera's landed on Mom in the front row, and Ellen addressed her. "You've must have known he was a special boy growing up?" She stated it in the form of a question.

Mom pulled down her mask to speak. "You know, it probably could have gone either way," she said. "If it weren't for the kindness of the woman who gave him shoes, this might be an entirely different story."

"That just goes to show how easily you can impact a child's life," Ellen said.

By the end of the eight-minute segment, we received a huge donation for Hav A Sole from Ellen's sponsors. That money would help us make it through another year.

Driving home, Mom and I felt exhilarated, and not just because she'd won a forty-four-inch television set, along with the rest of the audience, but because we got to experience the magical effect of Hav A Sole once again.

CORONAVIRUS

Our annual Thanksgiving dinner at my brother's house in 2020 had been canceled due to COVID-19. I was disappointed that I wouldn't be able to see my nieces and nephews or enjoy my sisters-in-law Erika's amazing turkey dinner. However, none of us wanted to take the chance of catching the virus.

The following month I received a frantic call from Mom. "Jerry is in liver failure."

"What?"

"He's in the emergency room, and they won't let Erika in because of the coronavirus." She started to sob.

I felt as though all the air had been sucked out of my body. "He'll be okay, Mom," I reassured her, but inside I was scared. We hadn't even finished grieving my brother's best friend, who had just passed away. Now Jerry was in the emergency room in the middle of a pandemic. His liver and kidney levels were off the charts. A sense of powerlessness gripped me and kept me awake all night.

The next day, Jerry tested positive for COVID-19 and was placed in an isolation ward. Mom called again. "We need to pray for your brother. He's got bad asthma."

"Believe me," I said. "I've been praying."

I thought back to the nineties, when Mom and I had lived in transitional housing. During my teens, my brother was either locked up or living somewhere else. But after serving time for assault, he got out of prison and was able to get his shit together. Now we were close, and I visited him and his family whenever I could. I was extremely proud of Jerry because he was the type of father who showed up to all the school functions and his kids' games. He couldn't be sick. His family still needed him, and I needed him as well.

Later that day, test results revealed that stones were blocking Jerry's gallbladder. His whole system was shutting down, and he needed surgery to remove his gallbladder. However, nothing could be done while he still had the virus. Intravenous antibiotics helped stabilize him. The hospital was short on beds, so he was sent home with a PICC line, and a nurse was ordered to come by every day. But twenty-four hours later, Jerry spiked a fever again and was back in the ER.

At home in my bed, I stared at the ceiling while fear hung like a black cloud over my head. I imagined my older brother in that bright, sterile hospital with the nurses too busy to give him proper care. If it wasn't for COVID-19, the family would have been there by his side. Mom had tried FaceTiming him a couple of times, but it was hard for him to talk. "I could see the fear in his eyes," she told me. "He can barely finish a sentence without getting out of breath."

I wanted to do something to fix it, but there was so much in my life that I couldn't control. I couldn't control the pandemic. I couldn't control my brother's health. I couldn't control Mom's fear of losing her eldest son. And I couldn't control my mind's repetitive loop of worst-case scenarios. Meanwhile, the minutes, hours, and days dragged on. The only deaths I had known were that of my grandmother and her husband, Paul, but they had lived long, full lives.

Fortunately, a week later, Jerry passed the stones. His blood work returned to normal, and he was finally able to go home. It took a month of bed rest for him to fully recover enough to undergo surgery and have his gallbladder removed.

Jerry being sick was one of those wake-up calls that reminded me just how fragile life is. After that, I knew I had to spend as much time with him as possible.

ROAD-TRIPPING

My brother had fully recovered when we went on our first Hav A Sole road trip together. We drove across the United States delivering shoes in four major cities. The long hours on the open highway gave us an opportunity to reflect on our childhood.

"Remember that fort I made in the backyard?" Jerry asked.

Jerry was twelve and I was four when he and his best friend, TJ, built an amazing fortress. They gathered up pieces of plywood and cardboard and constructed walls and a roof; they even brought pillows inside. It was a boys-only club tucked away in the corner of our backyard. I was the annoying little brother who wanted to hang out with the big guys. Inside, they would make up stories about imaginary intruders attacking us and how we'd have to fight to the bitter end to protect our castle.

"I fell and busted my lip inside that fort," I said.

Jerry laughed. "Oh, that's right."

"Mom got mad because I had to get stitches."

"Do you remember when they sent me to live in Texas for that year?" Jerry asked.

"Whoa, I forgot about that."

"Yeah. I was thirteen and pissed off, so they sent me to Uncle Doodie. I actually did well while I was living with him."

Uncle Doodie was the nickname we'd given to Dad's brother, Albert.

"Are you still mad at Mom and Dad?" I asked.

"Not anymore."

I asked him why. He said, "When I found out about Mom's own childhood and how her mother committed suicide, it helped me understand why she acted the way she did."

I nodded. "Yeah, that must have been hard for her."

Until Mom got sober, neither of us had known that she had had an unstable childhood, that her own mother was mentally ill, and that her father was an alcoholic. When she finally started talking about her past, it was easier to understand why she used drugs. And when she wrote her memoir, it revealed all the secrets her family had kept as a result of her mother's suicide. Thinking about all the generations of mental illness, alcoholism, and addiction in our family tree, it was a miracle we'd come out the other side.

As the sun disappeared over the horizon, I felt a deep sense of gratitude wash over me.

"We should do a road trip with all my kids," Jerry said.

"I'm going up to Oakland and Portland soon."

"Could you do it during spring break?"

I liked the idea of bringing my nieces and nephews to show them firsthand what Hav A Sole was all about. "Sure," I said.

***

It was still dark the morning of March 27 when we climbed into the van with me in the driver's seat. Jerry hopped in the passenger side while my two nephews, Marc, who was now eighteen, and Matthew, sixteen, sat in the back. My nieces, twenty-two-year-old Alyssa and twenty-one-year-old Mariah, followed behind us in another car.

As we drove out of Los Angeles, we were all in good spirits. I tapped on the wheel as rap music pumped out from the speakers and we headed to Oakland, in Northern California. Part of the fun of doing road trips was updating our social media accounts with our adventures, so we planned on finding some open basketball courts in parks to play a little ball. Both the boys were athletes and played on their high school varsity team. We stopped at two basketball courts to play a little game called 21, and we posted it on Instagram.

Five hours after leaving Los Angeles, we huddled together on a platform to watch the elephant seals flop around on the beaches of Peidras Blancas in San Simeon, Northern California. We fed friendly squirrels before driving up to Big Sur.

The sky was gray as we headed down a trail to Pfeiffer Beach. The sand had a tinge of purple, with views of stunning sea stacks and rock formations.

"Look at that, kids," Jerry said, pointing to the famous keyhole arch, a tunnel that opens up on the other side.

I had watched Jerry morph into a tender, doting father over the years, and I loved seeing his excitement as he introduced his kids to new places. A new feeling had begun to stir inside me ever since I had become engaged to Kara seven months earlier. The clock was ticking, and I wanted to have kids.

By the time we arrived at our Airbnb in the Bay Area, I was exhausted. Everyone claimed their beds and passed out for the night.

The next morning we all drove to San Francisco. I maneuvered the van up a steep, winding road and pulled into the parking lot of Twin Peaks, a world-famous tourist attraction with spectacular views of the Bay Area. I grabbed one of my cameras out of the back of the van and left the rest of my equipment inside. Standing several feet away from the van, I took a couple of family photos.

When I returned to the back of my van, the rest of my equipment was gone. It happened so quickly. "Shit! My camera bag is gone," I said. Thieves must have snuck back there.

"That's so fucked up, man," Jerry said.

My nieces and nephews also felt bad. "I'm so sorry, Uncle Rikki," Matthew said. "That's so messed up."

Somehow I remained calm on the outside, but inside I was beating myself up for leaving the door unlocked. *Why hadn't I locked the van? How could I have been so careless?* Maybe it was karmic debt from when I used to break into cars as a teen. I was finally seeing what it was like to be on the receiving end of theft.

When we got back to the Airbnb, my brother said, "I really appreciated how you handled yourself in front of the kids."

"Getting angry wasn't going to help anything," I said. It made me realize how much I had changed since starting Hav A Sole eight years earlier. Over time, I had learned how to accept things. I knew that getting pissed off would only lead to me being unhappy, and being with my family, I had a lot to be grateful for.

The next day we headed over to the Covenant House in Oakland. The moment we started giving out shoes, I forgot about my own problems. What filled my heart the most was watching my nieces and nephews hand out shoes. To instill in them the sense of giving back, something that took me so long to learn, made me feel proud. After giving out over fifty pairs of shoes, they were ecstatic.

As we crossed the Oakland Bay Bridge, the city grew smaller in my rearview mirror, and a sadness weighed on my chest as I remembered that I was leaving my camera gear behind.

I DO

May 14, 2022

The venue was a Spanish-style adobe house with a 1930s flair nestled in the Hollywood hills. Palm trees jutted skyward, framing an incredible view of the city. A steep driveway led to an internal courtyard, and beyond that was a swimming pool surrounded by tables.

The ceremony was set to take place in the courtyard, a moody haven where a jazzed-up fireplace was surrounded by arched pillars. An intricate blue mosaic tile was the central focal point on the floor. To one side was a bar, and on the other was a staircase that led to a wraparound balcony where guests could watch the ceremony from above.

I escorted Mom down the center aisle to sit beside Kara's mother and stepfather. I then joined my friend Chad, the pastor, up front.

As members of the wedding party, including Kara's friends, her brothers, and my nieces and nephews, came down the aisle, guests applauded and cheered as if hailing the starting lineup of their favorite basketball team. Finally, Jerry, my best man, entered and stood right beside me.

My breath caught in my throat a few minutes later when I saw Kara appear at the top of the stairs dressed in a sleeveless white lace wedding gown with a sweeping train and veil. She held a bouquet of daises and yellow sunflowers in her left hand. The afternoon sun bathed her in a golden light, and an overwhelming sense of love welled up in my chest.

Kara's stepfather met her at the bottom of the stairs and walked her down the aisle toward me. I shook his hand before taking Kara's hand in mine. We gazed into each other's eyes.

Pastor Chad then spoke. "Why are we really here today? For the party?"

Everyone laughed.

"No. Just kidding," he said. "Love is what brings us together today. To celebrate these two incredible human beings who fell madly in love with each other."

Chad looked from Kara to me. "Love is so good, but it's scary too. If you love deeply, you might be wounded. But there are no wounds that love cannot heal. You two are stepping into this crazy thing called marriage today and choosing a journey that can be full of obstacles, challenges, and difficulties. Isn't it crazy? Are you sure you want to do it?" Chad joked. "No. *It is* too late. We're going to do this."

It was time for our vows. "Kara," I said, "I promise to love you, to encourage you, and to trust you. I accept you exactly as you are, and I offer myself in return. I will care for you and always stand beside you. I realize at times your past was unstable and unpredictable. I know this because mine was too. But everything we've been through has led us to this point. I ask you to join me in being the best husband and wife we can be. Let's have a family and raise beautiful children in undeniable and unconditional love. I love you, and our future starts right now."

Kara then spoke. "This moment in my life is the definition of pure joy. Love didn't come easily for me. I had a very long list of failed relationships. I was often rejected. Even you rejected me at the beginning, but I knew you'd come around—or I'd find you. But today love has a new meaning in my life because of you. I always thought I had to earn someone's love, but you showed me that love is true freedom. Choosing you was the best decision I ever made. God has made me feel seen through your eyes. I promise from this day forward to do my best to keep God in the center of our lives."

Everyone applauded.

All that was left was the exchanging of our rings and Chad announcing that we were husband and wife.

I slowly lifted Kara's veil and we kissed, her hands gently holding my face. This was the woman I wanted to spend the rest of my life with. This was my wife.

Later, when Kara and I sat side by side at the sweetheart table by the pool, I looked around at all the people who were there. Dad, Mom, my brother, nieces and nephews, Kara's family, old and new friends. I felt surrounded by so much love. I was overwhelmed with gratitude.

When I think back to when my family broke up, all I longed for was to have everyone reunited again. Although it would take many years to get there, my wish finally came true at my wedding. Everyone was perhaps a little more weary, and we were all older, but everyone was still in the game.

My wedding may represent the ending of this book, but outside of these pages, it is also a new beginning. I am excited to see how the next chapter unfolds.

PHOTO ALBUM

Gary Drake & Rikki

Rikki delivers sneakers to a boy with large holes

A helping hand on skid row

Wendy Adamson (aka Mama Sole)

Hav A Sole event

Stay Home & Stay Active program

Hav A Sole Road Trip with Rikki & Jerry Mendias

Grateful woman receiving new sneakers

Twins at Miriam's House get new sneakers

Hav A Sole event with Steve and Kara as volunteers

Steve Simon at Covenant House

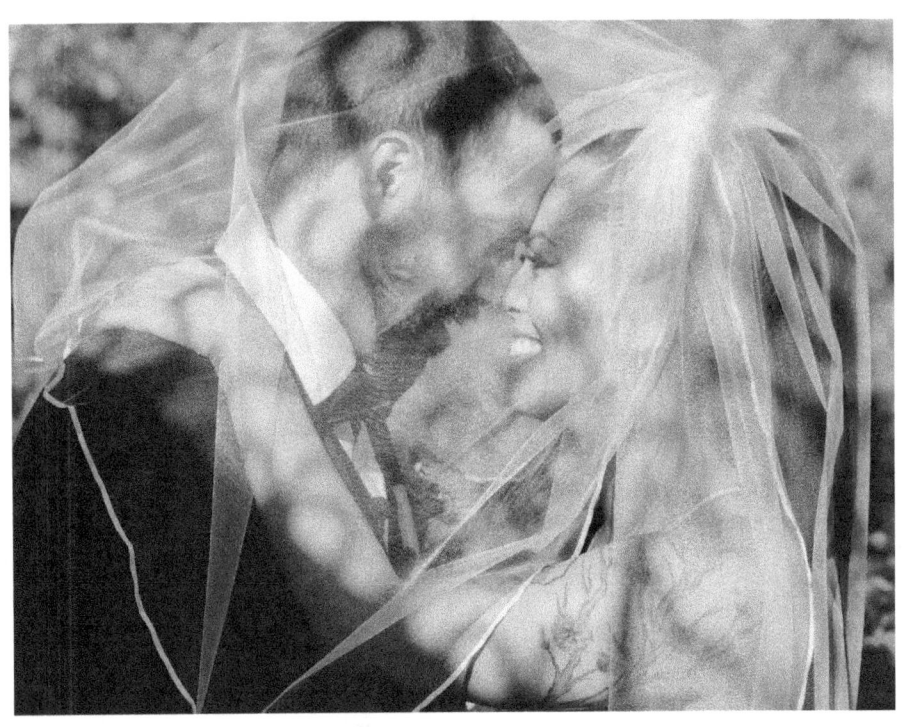

Rikki & Kara's Wedding

ACKNOWLEDGMENTS

It took a village to get me where I am today, which is why first and foremost I have to thank my mom, who not only believed in me, but believed that Hav A Sole's story needed to be told. If not for her focus and discipline, this book wouldn't exist.

Thank you to my beautiful wife, Kara, for joining me on this journey, and to my big brother, Jerry, for being a constant inspiration and reminding everyone that we are not our history and that people can change. Thank you to my father, who had the courage to make amends and bring healing to our relationship. And to my nieces and nephews, it is truly an honor to be your uncle. I am so proud of you.

I want to thank Gary Drake for taking a chance on a young knucklehead. His love and mentorship through my younger years helped mold me into the man I am today. I am grateful to you for walking me through the fire. To Geoff Farr, another solid role model in my life, and Cathi Carlton, whose support helped set me on the right path.

Thank you to my dear friend Marc Knopf for your friendship and the creative talents that you have generously shared since the inception of Hav A Sole.

Thank you to the Hav A Sole's board of directors, who continue to elevate our mission, and to all the volunteers who have helped us through the years.

A special thanks to the entire Simon family and to the Herbert Simon Family Foundation. We are deeply indebted to you. And last but not least, my deepest heartfelt gratitude to Steve Simon for championing Hav A Sole. Every pair of shoes we have given away and every life we have touched is the direct result of your unwavering belief in Hav A Sole. Without you, none of this would be possible. Thank you!

ABOUT THE AUTHORS

Rikki Mendias is a speaker, entrepreneur, and the founder and Executive Director of Hav A Sole, a nonprofit that has been delivering sneakers to underserved communities in Los Angeles and throughout the United States since 2014. Rikki is passionate about sneakers, basketball and photography, but more importantly, he is committed to having a positive impact on those around him.

Wendy Adamson is a writer, a motivational speaker, and an advocate for mental health. As a published author, Wendy has two books, *Mother Load* and *Incorrigible* where she documents her own struggles with addiction and the long arduous journey of healing that came as a direct result of getting sober.

havasole.com
IG: @havasole
www.facebook.com/havAsole

wendyadamson.com